Barking Up a Dead Horse

Avoiding the Wasted Time and Effort in Business-to-Business Sales

Tom Batchelder

A DIFFERENT APPROACH TO SALES AND PERSONAL ACHIEVEMENT

dog ear
PUBLISHING
First published by:
Dog Ear Publishing
4010 W. 86th Street, Ste H
Indianapolis, IN 46268
www.dogearpublishing.net

ISBN: 978-159858-850-7
Library of Congress Control Number applied for

This book is printed on acid-free paper.
Printed in the United States of America

Be Yourself, Sell More

If you are looking for or dealing with any of these things, you might be in the right place:

- Desire to get and keep more clients
- Feel like your people are not skilled at generating new business
- Your selling/prospecting process stretches out much too long
- Your organization is not doing an adequate job communicating your unique value to prospects and clients
- Need to increase morale, and team performance
- New ways to differentiate, less getting beat up on price
- Too many lingering, "on the fence" deals
- Non-sales staff (project managers, account executives, tech experts) need to do a better job at identifying new business opportunities from existing clients
- You get caught "doing the work" and don't make time for networking, prospecting
- Not growing at the rate you feel you deserve and desire

Testimonials

"Of all the past company training I have had, something was missing for me. I was introduced to the principles in this book and Tom's coaching at just the right time. Now, I really feel connected to my work, and finally feel that I have the processes, resources and tools to succeed."
— Dawn Muller, Sales Representative

"Since applying these principles, my income has tripled. Now, this is not a *quick fix*. My largest month before implementing this new approach was $45,000 in sales. Within eight months, I had a $180,000 month. My best year ever before was $235,000 in revenue. We are six months into this year and I currently have $900,000 in deals to close in my pipeline. I have learned to differentiate myself from my competition, and how not to get caught competing just on feature, function, and price."
— Brandon Jeffress, National Account Manager

"I have read through many sales training books. Yours was the first that actually talked about getting "sales-speak" OUT of our language, learning how to really connect with prospects, and get to the truth. This approach has taught me to overcome my fears and 'detach' my emotions so I can be the most effective in helping prospective clients solve problems. I am beginning to reach my true potential, as a person, business owner, and sales professional."
— Paul Lorinczi, Business Owner

"Over the last eight months of approaching sales in a new way, I have accomplished the following: Hit my annual quota in 6 months. Increased my average deal size from $40,000 to $250,000. Hit $1,000,000 in sales in eight months. Nearly doubled my income."
—Bill Crouch, National Sales Director

"In the end, that is the real work of an explorer: to share all that you have learned, to make it available to others, and to close that cycle that you started when you began your journey."

— Dr. Robert D. Ballard,
oceanographer and discoverer of the wreck of the Titanic

To Lisa,

You have supported my vision
and this unorthodox journey from day one.
I could not do what I do without you.

CONTENTS

ACKNOWLEDGEMENTS

I first want to thank my clients, current and past. Without them, this book would not be possible. It would be a bunch of theories and disjointed ideas rolling around in my head. I appreciate the trust you place in me and this unique approach to business communication and personal achievement. A special thanks to those of you (you know who you are) who have been staunch advocates for years, have continued to encourage me to write this book, and challenged me to step up to do my part to reach a larger audience.

Thanks to my Perficency team. (Perficency is a sales and leadership effectiveness organization that I founded in 2002.) Ray Green, Andrew Bogdan, Maryann Dolzani, Shawn Green, Shawn Hurt, Sara Hill, Kim McDaniels. It is because of this growing team that I am able to help more and more people communicate, lead, and sell in a different way. Without your faith in me and highly competent work in the field, I would not feel so inspired (or so pressured!) to write this book. To Dustin Brann, my editor, whose attention to detail helped make my "thinking out loud" more coherent for anyone that doesn't live inside my head.

Thanks to Bill Caskey, who first introduced me to a number of the underlying concepts I will be sharing with you. His book *Same Game, New Rules* broke ground for me and showed me that there was a new way to sell and room for a more sophisticated approach to business communication. Thank you to Bryan Neale, Adam Taisch, and Ron Taisch for your initial business support and encouragement that ultimately led to the completion of this book. I am grateful for the support and push received along the way from people such as Bob Petrello, Jonathan Hart, John Pearson, and Greg Neveu. The origins of this work and my organization came in part from the support of my visionary friend Azi Tabachnik who always challenged me to think bigger. To my family for their active support and encouragement: Lynne & Chuck Thompson, Mary & Jim Rice, John Batchelder, Edith Leech, Susan Loucks, Jim & Marion Tarr.

To Guy Hart and Bryce Whiting, who were a part of my initial journey to build an organization around the principles in this book. I know you will always be champions of a different approach to sales and business communication. I respect you and your approach to business and life.

And finally, to my young son, Nicholas. Every day I get out of bed, you are my inspiration.

INTRODUCTION

I had an old boss whose brain worked so fast he could mix and mangle a metaphor or catchphrase like nobody I had ever heard. When we were working on a title for the book, I threw out **Barking Up a Dead Horse**, half jokingly, in his honor and it stuck. This mixed metaphor has been eliciting immediate reactions from people from day one — from dazed confusion to spontaneous laughter. The more I thought about it, *Barking Up a Dead Horse* seemed like the perfect analogy to what I see happening for many business professionals, especially those in any sales or business development role. They are spending lots of time *Barking Up Wrong Trees* and equal amounts of energy *Beating Dead Horses*. I've seen staggering amounts of time and energy wasted because of unconscious thinking, habitual behaviors, ineffective written and spoken language, and inconsistent processes void of clear intent or straight forward next steps.

Professionals today spend as many as two thousand hours working over the course of a year. Of those two thousand hours, research, straw polling, and my own personal experience tell me that most professionals are at their best, maximizing their strengths, optimally effective, laser focused, inspired, and producing positive results no more than 20 percent of the time. That leaves upwards of 1,600 hours, 80 percent of their time, or 200 work days annually, operating at sub par levels of effectiveness and efficiency. It isn't that people are just slacking off; in fact it's quite the contrary. The professionals I know are flying, driving, on conference calls, in client meetings, negotiating deals, answering requests for proposals, assembling flashy PowerPoints, gaming out a strategy for the next big deal, filling out forms, answering hundreds of emails, making phones calls, and thinking about work most of their waking hours.

Working harder is not the problem. Having access to more information is not the issue. Every day we get inundated with information, much of which we never asked for and isn't in our own best interest to consider. Let's face it; the majority of professionals today are addicted to activity. At the same time, they are often unclear about what they are doing and why they are doing it. Despite all of their efforts, their new business approach is unfocused and often leads to getting lied to. In their minds, they are underestimating their own true value to others. In their written and spoken words they are not effectively communicating what differentiates them from the competition. This in turn makes it harder for new clients to buy even if they do have a genuine need. Business professionals today are too often unclear and don't have the highest intent entering into important meetings, presentations, and negotiations. They are lacking a consistent, disciplined client engagement process that attracts the right kinds of clients and helps alert them of when to walk away from bad business. More often, they are not really listening and they are missing the tangible clues and subtle psychological cues that can provide an extra edge in a negotiation. Many are playing a role, putting on a mask, and not really being their true selves. Much of this is driven by the fear of losing a client or a new "big" deal. This fear keeps them from asking important qualifying questions and having the right mindset to ensure they find and close the right kinds of new business opportunities.

I know this sounds kind of grim. The good news is that there is hope. There are successful, disciplined, well-intended business professionals out there who are having success. They are doing it with more effective, sustainable, forward-thinking approaches to negotiation, new client engagement, and business and personal growth. And although change is hard, we all have the capacity to "rewire" our brains, adopt new techniques and interrupt tired, ineffective approaches to our business results and life success.

I like to visit bookstores and wander the aisles, looking for inspiration and new thinking. With my multiple interests in business, sales, leadership, communication, and psychology, there is plenty to choose from. I have found a number of unique works that inspired new thinking while also providing useful information relevant to me and my world. And yet among the few books that do speak to me I still find myself looking for something more. Mostly I find more of the same dense, corporate, process-oriented rhetoric or cute, warm and fuzzy metaphors designed to dramatically change my life in one sitting. They are all well-meaning, useful, and many are written by smart, well credentialed experts. That being said, I have long sensed there is still a gap in the conversation.

What I find, especially in the *sales* section, is that there isn't much that speaks to the heart of how and why so many people who are responsible for developing new business get sapped of energy, focus, and inspiration over time. Aside from having a "system" for how to get from point A to point B, most don't talk honestly about the struggles we have in our professional lives, and the fear we have of change and not getting what we want. There is little discussion about the power that authentic confidence, a disciplined mindset, and consistent high intent can have on the bottom line of profit and productivity. Seldom are words like fear, courage, ego, and personal growth mixed together for a professional audience looking for more effective ways to grow their business. There are many books full of information, anecdotes, and inspiring stories, but do they really stimulate new thinking?

It is time for a new wave of creative, forward-thinking, thoughtful leaders in sales, business communication, and life achievement that are NOT promising the silver bullet. Coaches, consultants, authors, and speakers that are moving beyond the small minded pep rally, the self-serving academic gathering, and the religious fervor stirred by following one mega-famous talking head offering "the path to success, riches, and happiness." I have found there is a hunger for new leaders that are serving a professional audience and delivering practical solutions blended with creativity and connecting to a deeper level of substance and, dare I say, soul. This movement is small, but happening, driven by a select group of progressive leaders as well as thoughtful consultants, coaches, speakers, and authors who provide unique and valuable outside perspectives.

I have had the pleasure to meet, train, coach, and consult with thousands of good people in the business world. They want to make money and at the same time find a way to also make a difference in the world. They are successful, highly intelligent, creative, empathetic, and good communicators. They are also getting burned out and tired of all the ego-posturing and corporate b.s. These good people are seeking more productive ways of **thinking** and **being** in their work life. Most of them have what I call a high "Courage Quotient" and are willing to rock the boat in the name of meaning and growth. They are hungry to help grow organizations, develop leaders, and build teams that practice what they preach, and also have the courage to speak and act with integrity and radical, thoughtful honesty. They want their work to have meaning, challenge them to face their fears, and push them to new levels of learning, growth, and financial abundance. These are people with an uncommon level of commitment, perseverance, and passion. Some of them have found careers where this gets to show every day, and others have it bottled up within them, ready to burst.

This book is about new ways to think, talk, and execute an approach to attract more of the right kinds of new clients and business opportunities. It offers a larger philosophical framework and specific, proven examples of how to get better results, without wasting so much time and energy. In addition, I am interested in helping growth oriented professionals become more conscious and sophisticated about how their approach to engaging prospects and clients can help them not only in business but in their personal lives as well.

If nothing else, I trust you will find an interesting collection and arrangement of thoughts, guiding principles, and tangible ideas that will challenge your status quo.

It is a scary, dynamic, and incredibly exciting time in our world. There is more abundance than ever before for many, but also more scarcity, fear, and anxiety. A new wave of tolerance for mediocrity and resistance to change seems to have taken root. I offer this book to inspire and challenge others to passionately pursue a commitment to interrupting unproductive patterns, create sustainable change, and generate significant, quantum leaps in results.

Be curious. Have fun. Do and say courageous things.

Take care,
Tom Batchelder
tom@perficency.com

July, 2007

Barking Up a Dead Horse

WHAT TO EXPECT FROM READING THIS BOOK

Warning: There is no magic fairy dust within these pages.
I do not believe you can follow any magical path to riches
and success. What I am suggesting is difficult to consistently
practice, and yet elegantly simple in theory. Before reading
further, I need to give you a few disclaimers.

1. I do not have "The answer." This is not a connect-the-dots
"how to become a better salesperson in 30 days" manual. Some of these
principles and approaches you may already know and understand, but are not consistently practicing. Other elements
might be new to you. These days most people are increasingly
looking outside of themselves for answers. There are plenty
of authors, speakers, and "gurus" that would like to give you
"the answer." Related to the topics in this book I do not have
an easy answer for you. I do have some ideas, concepts, and
approaches that have worked for me and thousands of others.
There is no one "right way" to sell, negotiate, communicate,
and achieve. The real answers are already within you buried
just beneath the surface.

2. I will not be attempting to name-drop or entertain. I will
give you a few samples, examples, and templates from both
my experiences and those of real people who are having success out in the business world with the material presented in
this book. I am not, however, going to tell you the story of how
Jack Welch used what I taught him to win an $800 million
project for GE on the day of his retirement (For the record – I
don't know Jack). These kinds of anecdotes and case studies

can be inspiring and interesting. The problem I have with this star-studded approach is that it can make it too easy for you to separate yourself from being able to do what these already powerful, rich, and seemingly super smart people can do. I will not try and sell you on how impressive my company is or how super important my clients are. I am going to share with you some examples of how others and I have applied this material. These people struggle with the same things you do.

3. This book alone is just the beginning. Access to and processing information is one thing. It can be helpful, but limited, in its ability to generate sustainable change and quantum leaps in results. I believe most well intended efforts at sales and business communication training are destined for mediocre results at best; a complete waste of time and money at worst. In order to create real, sustainable change in individual and organizational results, you must:

- Re-think and rebuild the foundation of all sales-related thinking, language, and processes.
- Integrate a new approach slowly and consistently over a period of time.
- Blend small group training with some form of one-to-one coaching and real-time, situational support.
- Have complete, hands-on participation from key leadership / company stakeholders.

This material, like anything else, is only effective if you are practicing and experientially building it into your day-to-day interactions. If you want to get more from this material, start a discussion group with your team or incorporate some of these practices into your weekly meetings. Consider hiring a coach or consultant to help you delve deeper into these topics and make them specifically relevant for your business.

4. You will experience repetition. There are a number of points, and key concepts that you will find repeated throughout the book. This is by design, for two reasons. The first reason is that the fundamental concepts run more like undercurrents through everything you will read. They are the glue that holds all the elements of the book together. Secondly, I find the only way to re-train your brain is through repetition. It's difficult to think new thoughts and shift your approach in a sustainable way. The only hope for this is repetition and consistent daily application.

5. You may not agree. You may find there are concepts, ideas, and philosophies presented in this book that you don't agree with or can't quite wrap your brain around. It is not my intention to have you believe everything that I believe. I am going to suggest to you some tangible tools and intangible ideas that have significantly impacted bottom line results for thousands of other people, including me. You must decide what's useful for you and what you're open to. Our human tendency to avoid conflict and not share differing opinions in a respectful dialogue significantly limits our ability to learn and grow. I'll be curious to hear what you connect with and get results from, as well as what you most dislike, or don't agree with in these pages. All feedback is welcome: tom@perficency.com or www.perficency.com/barking

INTENT AND OVERVIEW

The principles in this book are fairly straightforward. I believe that we all make the whole process of "sales" or "business development" much too difficult, and thus extremely inefficient. What is most astounding to me is how difficult it is for most individuals and organizations to recognize, accept, and correct these inefficiencies on their own.

Because the principles I am suggesting are so clear-cut, they can inspire resistance. I have found many in business and sales who think they "got it" and find these approaches to be simplistic and not relevant to their work. Some have judged my approach as a bunch of psychological mumbo jumbo. They say, "Just work harder and stop your whining."

People are by nature risk averse and want to feel in control at all times. Everything I will outline in these pages is designed to help you maintain greater control over your process of new business development. It is also intended to reduce the amounts of lost time and energy and the risk of having not enough of the right kinds of business on the books or in your pipeline. The paradox here is that you first have to be willing to let go of control and admit you don't have all the answers.

"While many corporations today are beginning to realize the increasing importance of sustained innovative ability as a competitive necessity, many will find it difficult to adopt the central proposition of this book. It is not that the changes effected by the new procedures are too complex or strange — in the deepest sense, they are nothing if not natural — but they appear to threaten and run counter to familiar tactics for retaining control and avoiding risk."

— Jerry Hirshberg, Author of The Creative Priority
& founder of Nissan Design International

Layered beneath your fears - *of talking to people you don't know, ...of rejection, ...of the unknown* and the ego's desire *...to be liked, ...to win, ... to be separate* - these principles are about reaching out. Reaching out to people - some that you know and some that you don't - to see if they are open to have a conversation. And doing so in such a way that gives you the best possible chance of getting the basic truth of every opportunity: "Yes I am interested in talking further, and am open to share what's going on for us to see if we might have a fit," -or- "No I am not, at this time."

If your prospect is open to talk with you, your approach will be focused on creating an environment where they are comfortable enough they are not going to be "sold" or "manipulated" that they will continue telling you the truth about their situation. As you get them to tell you the truth, then you have a window of opportunity to concisely and meaningfully communicate who you are, what you do, and why people decide to work with you. If you are doing your job effectively, you will quickly find out if there is enough of a "fit" to move to a next step.

Everything within these pages is designed to help you execute this simple premise, *get more truth from your prospects and you will waste less time*, with optimal effectiveness. If you are open to analyze your current approach to growing your business and are interested in making fundamental shifts in your thinking, you are in the right place.

Fundamental Issues and their Consequences

With the continued emergence of a more psychologically savvy culture, there is an opportunity for change in the world of traditional sales and business communication. The sales and business communication process is more complex than ever and many old techniques and ideas are becoming ineffective and obsolete. The new levels of knowledge and complexity for both buyers and sellers also open up new opportunities to do things differently and more effectively.

All of the business professionals and organizations I have worked with have their own unique set of challenges due to specific industry dynamics and their particular corporate culture. There are, however, three areas where I find most professionals consistently lacking in optimal effectiveness.

Issue 1: Not fully understanding, believing in, or effectively communicating your unique value. Most professionals and their organizations either unknowingly discount or don't understand their own unique value and thus underestimate what value they bring to the marketplace. When I speak of unique value, I mean the reasons beneath the surface buzzwords and corporate speak that make clients want to work with you and no one else. Some of your value is obvious (i.e.: the specific performance of your products, the high levels of service and expertise your people provide, etc.). However, much of the uniqueness of what you do and how you do it is hidden beneath the surface and needs to be brought out in order to more effectively communicate to your clients. The more you believe in and can be meaningfully articulate about your unique value, the less you will struggle with…

- An overall lack of differentiation and resulting commoditization of your product or service.
  Getting paid less for doing the same or more work.
- Getting caught competing in the "Request For Proposal" process where differentiation is difficult. Spending a significant amount of resources on opportunities that never come to fruition.
- Competing on price and negotiating from a "One down" position without any leverage or control.
- Fear of losing the business. Getting attached to the money in a way that hampers your ability to ask effective questions or negotiate from a position of equality.

Issue 2: Not having a client engagement process that allows you to be in control. This is relevant for processes related to engaging new prospects, re-engaging past clients, and developing more business from existing clients. Even if you have a formal company process in place, I find consistent, disciplined, day-to-day execution in the field is uneven. If you or your team are actually disciplined about your process, it is then the mental discipline (i.e.: ensuring you don't get too needy and emotionally attached) that often needs improvement, especially in high stakes situations. Without a clear and effective process that you control, you will get caught defaulting to the prospect's process. They will be the ones in control. You might have often assumed that if you don't follow every step of the prospect's process that you will lose your opportunity to win the business. I've found this usually turns out not to be true at all. Some of the symptoms of defaulting to the prospects process automatically...

- Getting caught negotiating primarily on price and other rational details.
- You are not privy to important details about your prospective new client and their process. (i.e.: when the decision will be made, who's making the decision, why they are doing this, why now, who cares, why they are considering you.)
- Getting so excited about just having the opportunity to be included in the process that you either forget or can't muster the courage to ask difficult questions that will help more quickly qualify your prospect.
- Process drags on for a long time. You are often the last to know where things are and what decisions have or haven't been made.

Issue 3: Emotional attachment to getting the business. This happens most often when you want and need the business more than your prospect needs to solve their problem. When you care more about closing the deal than you do about solving their problem, you get attached and lose control. You get excited and are too quick to move the process along before covering essential steps and learning the answers to key questions. When this happens, closing percentages plummet. Controlling the process, properly pacing it, and knowing when to move on and walk away is an essential discipline to attracting more of the right kinds of new business. Making sure you are never too far ahead of your prospect or wanting things more than they do will help minimize dealing with symptoms such as...

- Not getting phone calls or emails returned
- Losing status and perceived value from clients and prospects. They are put off by your actions such as calling or emailing too frequently, or how your tone of voice and message seems needy, even desperate.
- Deal is stalled or dead. Wasting your valuable time and energy on something that you got excited about too early. You've lost control yet are still counting on the deal in your projections.
- Not moving on. The energy and "headspace" you give your prospective deal that keeps you from moving on and looking for the next new prospect. Keeping you from more quickly attracting someone who has more of a sense of urgency, sees your value, understands their issues, wants to fix them, and is open to your help.

Now that we've uncovered the core issues and symptoms, let's lay the groundwork for framing the way you look at sales and your own achievement. Before we launch into some detailed elements of how to solve these issues, I think it's important to spend some time framing out our larger models for dealing with these issues.

Let's start with a big picture "macro" framework that drives the uncovering of fundamental inefficiencies in a company's approach to sales growth. The two categories we focus on here are: Strategy (rational brain) & Psychology (emotional brain).

Strategy

Competitive organizations develop arsenals of sharp presentations, snappy value propositions, competitive positioning statements, and ever changing deal structures to enable their sales force to go out there and "grow the business."

While key to overall growth, traditional strategic "Sales Enablement" alone generates inconsistent revenue growth. This is because sales people are inconsistent at the most important and leveragable point of execution: the customer interaction. Beyond traditional sales processes and closing techniques, sales people too often lack:

- An effective vocabulary to keep from being commoditized.
- The soft skills and confidence to accurately and quickly qualify a prospect.
- The awareness and discipline to keep large customers from unnecessarily stalling a sale.

Sustainable business growth requires a sales force to combine their strategic tools with the tactical skills of awareness, mental discipline, and language within a consistent, executable process. Otherwise, growth is limited by what is in effect the "last mile" issue for every sales organization: excellent enablement but inconsistent execution.

Psychology

As the gatekeeper to the rational part of our brain, our emotional brain first attaches an immediate "tag" (i.e.: threatening vs. safe, uncomfortable vs. reassuring) to every interaction and experience we have. The sequence of this "wiring" ensures that humans are emotional creatures first. This elegant structure ends up sabotaging us professionally because those emotional life experiences that we try (mostly unconsciously) each day to either avoid or repeat end up driving compulsive reactions to specific situations; often with unfortunate results.

In business, this emotional-rational conflict shows up intensely for those involved in buying, selling, and negotiating; activities that are commonly filled with emotions such as fear, excitement, and attachment.

Business leaders and sales professionals that have a better understanding of and disciplined control over their reactions are best positioned for accelerated, sustainable growth and bottom line results. You must be committed to and interested in a framework for a more honest and "human" approach to communication and collaboration. The end result will be higher quality business relationships, and quicker results, with less of the pain and conflict often associated with sales and negotiation.

The "micro" framework, which explains the foundation of how to execute more effectively toward growth, focuses on three primary elements: Thinking, Language, and Process. These operate both independently and in concert with one another. When combined, you give yourself the best possible chance for an exponential shift in results.

Thinking, Language, Process

Thinking, or mental discipline, is most simply defined as the ability to be emotionally aware (of any fear, or excitement) and detached (from wanting the business more than your prospect wants their problem solved). Your thinking drives your intent in all prospect interactions. If you are more focused on their money than their problems or in presenting your solution than uncovering their true needs and motives for change, you are operating from low intent and are out of control. This doesn't mean you won't close business, because you will (and do). It does mean that you're often not finding the right kind of business and are spending more time than you need to working on deals that end up going nowhere. Being more aware of and more disciplined about your thinking in all sales / business development situations is the first key to new levels of success.

> *"Successful companies are willing and able to uncover inefficiencies and turn them into opportunities."*

Language discipline is focused on the specific words you use in email, phone, and face-to-face communication. These words have the ability to keep people at ease, create an environment to get the truth, and to stay in control of each conversa-

tion. Discipline of language focuses on better understanding what key words and phrases are essential to keeping you in an equal position with prospects and clients, and what words and phrases put you in a one-down position that get you lied to and commoditize you. Language is also about being able to frame your value in a unique, compelling way that others can relate to.

- Thinking drives language.
- Language is the bridge that connects Thinking and Process.
- Key words / phrases to use (not use) in order to keep on an equal footing with prospects and clients.
- Language designed to get the truth.
- Framing all conversations, expectations up front. Ensuring that "no" is ok at each step.

Process discipline is about having a step-by-step process and guiding framework that you lead clients through. You must be clear which steps must not be skipped and when it is or is not appropriate to be flexible. Having the awareness to know when things are moving too fast and the discipline to know how and when to slow them down. And also when to (respectfully) walk away.

- Having a process for engaging new clients
  & getting more business from existing ones.
- Clarifying a next step at the end of every conversation.
- Following a system that allows individuals to be optimally effective, minimizing costly emotions (i.e.: fear, ego, attachment, etc.).
- Having discipline and confidence that your process is the best system for both you and your prospect to follow.

Now that I have framed out the *macro* and *micro* lenses through which to view these principles, there are also three fundamental *undercurrents* to identify. You will read more about these in the pages that follow, but because they are at times subtle, I want to point them out.

The first is the importance of being genuine; talking in a language and tone that cuts through the noise and b.s. of the typical *corporate speak / rah-rah / look at how smart I am* that is so common today. Stop playing that game. Be yourself.

The second is a fundamental shift from putting yourself in what I call a "one-down" position and communicating with prospects and clients from a position of equality. I have met very few people in business that do a good job of this.

Finally, we will talk about how people learn, grow, and change. This is relevant for you as a business professional, and also for understanding your prospect's mentality when they are looking to make a decision to change. The more you understand and embrace the opportunities to interrupt old patterns in order to create new results, the more effective you will also be at leading yourself and others through a healthy process of change.

Genuineness - You Can't Fake It

At the base of these elements to sales and business communication is what I call an undercurrent of genuineness. This is not something that you can fake or learn. Sometimes it's right beneath the surface, but is getting covered over by buzzwords, and your "professional self" that wants to sound impressive and super smart at every turn. This baseline is about stripping away all the layers of habits and mental programming that keep you from being more genuine and thoughtfully, radically honest in your business development conversations with new prospects and key clients. By "thoughtfully, radically honest" I mean to be yourself, talk like a regular human being, and to be direct in a humble yet bold way. Stop trying so hard. You can be yourself and sell your services at the same time. The two actually go hand in hand.

One-Down, One-Up, All Even

The over-arching framework for the principles in this book can be summarized by a very simple visual: v – V. It's what I like to call "little v – big V." It has been my experience that most people in any sales role (formal or informal) are unaware of the ways they put themselves in a one-down position with clients and prospects. For example, thinking, "They have the money and I want it; therefore, they are in charge." This one-down position comes in the form of thoughts that spill over into language and process. All of this ends with you or your team getting caught defaulting to following the prospect's process for engagement. Before we proceeded I thought it might be useful to have an overview tool to use as a filter for yourself or your team and how you're "showing up" with clients and prospects on a daily basis.

Exercise: Visualizing our Value
Positioning Ourselves within the Conversation

One-Down

Concept

Selling from weakness—a position of less than, "I'm just happy someone is talking to me and asking for a bid. Glad to just get a meeting."

You | Prospect/Client

V V

Language

"Please call me back."
"What do I need to do to get your business?"

Thinking

I'm not worthy.
Defaulting to their process.
Calling at the lowest levels.
Little belief in personal value.

One-Up

Concept

Selling features and benefits.
Talk 75% listen 25%.

Language

"We know we can really help you."

Thinking

"You're screwed up and need us."
No genuine empathy for situation
or person. It's all about selling.
"I can help everybody."

You   Prospect/Client

V | V

All Even

Concept

Selling from equality, believe in
your personal value, company
value and fit in the marketplace.
Talk 25%, listen 75%.

Language

"What I have found works best…"
"I need to know more before I can
   say we are a good fit."

Thinking

We can't help everybody, only those
open to help and exploring new
approaches to what they're currently
doing. Position of high intent, looking to solve problems, and not just
about closing the deal.

You   Prospect/Client

V | **V**

Opportunity to Interrupt Patterns

I have worked with numerous companies and individuals that are at pivotal points in their lifecycle. They are trying to reach the next level and the same old thinking and actions are not getting them there. They are open to new thinking about themselves, their value, and their approaches to selling and developing their people. There is missed opportunity that is causing them pain or specific things that are just not working. Something needs to change.

People are emotional creatures, not rational. My job is to help you, if you are open to it, interrupt old patterns and habits that don't serve you. In order to increase your results you must learn new ways of looking at your habits, of talking about your business, and of executing your process for engaging new clients more effectively. When you are able to make these changes, and execute more effectively over time, you begin to create new neuropathways. This actually re-wires your brain and your ability to duplicate new, more effective processes. This lays the foundation for sustainable change and more intuitive, natural execution.

There is a fine line to walk with much of what I'm suggesting in this book. The line between the approach to your thinking, language, and process that I suggest and manipulation is a thin one. Traditional sales and sales training often talk of the gamesmanship of sales. While my suggested approach to sales and growing your business could be seen as just another form of manipulation and gamesmanship, there is a difference. There is an underlying element of consciousness, goodwill, and high intent to do the right thing that keeps these approaches from being manipulative or subversive.

It's hard to do the things I suggest without having high intent. Your process will break down. Your ego will take control. People will see through the words and pick up on what's really going on behind them if you are pushy, overly controlling, or seem to be playing games. You can sell and negotiate the way you have always done it, which is fine if you're willing to accept the same results. Or, you can consider new ways of thinking about your business, communicating your unique value, effectively controlling the sales process, and spending your time and energy. With an authentic approach, enough goodwill, and a little extra business savvy, this material should help you to be more effective and fulfilled.

Now it's time to take a good look into the mirror, on to the assessment.

ASSESSMENT /
SELF-INVENTORY

*"A mirror has the quality of enabling a man to see his image in it,
but for this he must stand still."*
— Kierkegaard

*"Not only must you play a role in solving the problem, you must be able to
acknowledge and 'own' your contribution to the circumstances. In other
words, you will be more powerful in solving the problem when you understand
how your actions or inactions helped create the problem. The group may
share responsibility, but each individual must shoulder his or her piece."*
— Connors, Smith, Hickman, The Oz Principle

*"You find peace not by rearranging the circumstances of your life, but by
realizing who you are at the deepest level."*
— Eckhart Tolle, A New Earth

Slow Down

These days we are all guilty of moving too fast, falling victim
to the increasing complexity and velocity of our lives. Some of
this is the reality of life in the 21st century. Some of this is just
habit. Some of this is a defense mechanism; we are afraid to
slow down and miss an opportunity. A reality check seems too
intimidating; we're afraid of what a good look in the mirror
might reveal, both personally and professionally. So we keep
going.

This process is a chance to STOP and consider you might
have some habits and patterns in your life that might not
be serving your best interests. Maybe there are other ways to

approach finding and engaging new prospects, growing business from existing clients, and motivating yourself and those around you.

Carve out five uninterrupted minutes to fill in the assessment below. Don't overanalyze each question. Read it, sit for a second, and then go with your initial gut response. Does each statement ring true for you or does it seem far-fetched? The more honest you are with yourself up front, the more useful this book will be. The questions are formulated to correspond with the primary focus and teaching points of the book. Tally up your score at the end.

Assessing Your Business and Yourself

Answer each question on a scale of 1-10, 10 being mastery, 1 being struggle mightily.

___ I am clear and passionate about my job / career, what I do, and why I do it.

___ New business development activities energize me.

___ There are more than enough prospects out there for me; the marketplace is abundant.

___ I have a systematic process for finding and developing new business with new prospects and existing clients.

___ I am working on the right-sized prospective accounts that will fuel sustained growth.

___ I am focused and consistent with my new business development outreach.

___ I have no trouble getting to the true decision makers within an organization.

___ There is nothing uncomfortable or stressful about selling and negotiating.

___ I have no doubt about the value I bring to my clients and the marketplace.

___ I have no doubt about the premium value of my organization and the products / services we provide our clients.

___ I clearly understand what kinds of challenges my ideal clients are facing and looking to solve when they hire me.

___ I clearly understand what kinds of opportunities my ideal clients are looking to capitalize on when they hire me.

___ I am able to get new prospects to quickly trust me and open up about their challenges.

___ I feel like I am getting the truth and the whole story from new prospects about their business.

___ When I'm negotiating with prospects, there aren't any questions that I am uncomfortable asking.

___ I am always curious, looking to solve problems. With new prospects, I have the highest intent to see if I can help.

___ I'm open to the possibility that I might not be able
to help some prospects, or that they may not be open
to my help at this time.

___ I have turned down business before. I am not afraid
to walk away from bad business.

___ I never get too attached to deals and don't take "no"
personally.

___ I have a selling method and philosophy that allows me
to feel in control of the negotiating process with new
prospective clients.

___ I do not get commoditized and pressured to negotiate
on price.

___ My average sales cycle is the right amount length,
never dragging on too long.

___ I do not currently have any deals in the pipeline
that have stalled.

___ I have a high regard for my own personal value
and don't tolerate being treated unprofessionally
by existing clients or new prospects.

___ Business revenue and my personal income are at
the level that I want.

___ I receive the kind of support I need when working
on important, new opportunities. I am not doing
it alone.

___ I am comfortable asking for help when I need it.

___ I feel passionate and energized by my work.
There is no negative affect on my home life.

___ I am not afraid to take risks.

___ I have no doubt in my ability to reach my short term
and long term goals.

OK, you did it. Looking back at the questions and your answers, how do you feel about your current state? Really good? Really bad? Somewhere in between? Now, add up your score and write it here _____.

250-300: You are on track or already there. You are doing most of the right things. You have most likely found your niche and established momentum in your work and life. As with anything there is, of course, room for growth. Leveraging your strengths is often the best way to focus your time and attention at this level. Get even better at the things that you already do well. Use this material to add a few new tools and perspectives for both yourself and those on your team. If nothing else, you may find reminders of what you already know but sometimes forget in your daily rush.

200-250: Relative Mastery. Just as Tiger Woods decided, at the peak of his stellar professional golf career, to rework his technique, consider an overhaul of how you approach new business development. Look at what you might need to change in order to make a quantum leap in your income and overall effectiveness. Consider ways to avoid burnout and re-energize yourself and your efforts to grow your business. Look at any long held beliefs about yourself, your business, and the marketplace that might be limiting your ability for next level achievement.

150-200: Strong. You possess a strong foundation of overall business and sales-specific experience. There are still inefficient patterns blocking your ability to reach the next level of success and fulfilment. It may be that you need to be more disciplined and systematic about your process and approach for developing new business. The biggest challenge at this stage is often becoming more aware of your thought-patterns. Better understanding your emotions (i.e.: avoidance, attachments, fears) will help you be even more effective with your time and energy. It will also help you close more of the right kinds of new business. Willpower and hard work can help you get to this point. It cannot alone take you to the next step of your own growth and achievement. Take a look at the areas where you scored yourself lowest. These are ideal starting points for change.

100-150: Time to commit to change. If you fall in this area, you are at risk of losing yourself in what I call *"no man's land,"* which leads to going through the motions without any sense of purpose or passion behind your actions. You may be unsure of which direction to point your career and where to focus your energy. Major shifts are needed: shifts in your thinking, daily focus, and sustained effort. In order to do this and get re-energized, you may need to make a job or career change. If radical changes are out of the question, then shifts in your thinking about yourself and attitude about your job are a good place to start. If any of this rings true, you would also benefit from a coach, counselor, or some other type of peer support / accountability group to assist you in your quest to be more effective at work and fulfilled in your life.

Below 100: Help needed. If you score below 100, you are in the wrong job, career path, or company. If you feel that you are in the right work environment, it may just mean that you are in a new role and in an intense transition period with a steep learning curve. It might be that you're having a really bad day or month at work. Either way, your current situation and mindset are not sustainable, at least not if you want to be happy, healthy, enjoy your work, and make more money. Something needs to change. As you read further, identify the most important shift that needs to happen for you — either in your thinking or your specific approach to your job. Use this material to clarify and focus your plan moving forward. Enlist others close to you to help support you in this time of transition. Challenge yourself to make changes that are sorely needed.

This analysis is far from scientific, however, it has proven to be a useful assessment of current mindsets and overall approaches to new business development. My suggestion would be to find three key areas for improvement and develop a plan around these to improve your mindset, process, and results. Use this as a guide for what areas you focus on mostly in the chapters ahead. The more targeted and clear you are about what you need to improve, the more you will get out of this book.

To achieve real gains from this assessment, you should revisit it in 30 days and see what has improved. This assessment is meant to grow with you. Ideally, you will assess yourself, and your team if you have one, every 90 days. Do this consistently for a year and you will see significant changes in both tangible bottom line and intangible results. You can download fresh copies of this assessment at www.perficency.com/assessment.

WHAT'S DRIVING IT ALL?
THE BIGGER PICTURE

Making the case for new ways of looking at our Thinking, Language, and Process for all new business development efforts.

Before we get into more ground-level issues and application of my suggested approaches to more effective thinking, language, and sales process strategy, I wanted to offer three larger perspectives that helps keep all of this content in context.

Increasing Interconnectedness

Although this headline is a chance for a *Cumbaya* moment, that is not my intention (Please save all group hugs for the end of the book). My intent is to highlight our interconnectedness in this global economy, geopolitical scene, and through mass media delivered around the world in milliseconds. I believe the reality of our communication and technological connectedness also has a greater impact on the weight and consequences of our actions. As we see playing out on the national and international news on a daily basis, our thoughts, beliefs, words, and actions can have an immediate impact felt by millions. We are creating ripples that come back to us in many ways - some exciting and positive and others disturbing.

The overall public image of our corporate culture, corporate leaders, and political leaders is at a low point. People are skeptical, untrusting, and tired of what they judge to be voices of greed and hypocrisy.

"Fewer than half of all Americans have a favorable opinion of business today...
Business became disconnected from their fundamentals, producing "perceived
value" instead of real value, because that's what the stock market rewards."
— Fortune Magazine, New Rules for Winning
by Betsy Morris, July 2006

I was at a workshop recently where the speaker, a well-known leadership consultant, talked about a client describing his company culture. He described it as being *"In a state of advanced lip service."* The funny and cutting *Dilbert* jokes aside, it seems this is as good a time as any to acknowledge and work on cutting out the lip service, getting more real, and acknowledging the impact our thoughts, language, and actions have on those around us.

Guanxi is a Chinese word that when translated means *networks of mutually beneficial relationships essential to success.* The most successful individuals, teams, and organizations of the 21st century are and will be developing and leveraging their networks of relationships with integrity, transparency, accountability, and mutual benefit.

As evolving, creative human beings, we are all hungry to feel like our lives make a difference. However, there is a lack of material written about the soul in the corporate world. It seems that if you can't put it in a box or on a spreadsheet, most don't want to talk about it. While there has been progress made on this subject in the workplace in the past ten years, there still is a lack of humanity and sanity in the high stakes world of sales, negotiation, and business growth.

Our lives are all connected. There is no real separation between us. When we think of the person sitting across the table - whether a prospect, client, boss, or business partner - as connected to us, there is a better chance we will be able to listen intently and talk honestly without ego-posturing or playing games. Most people can see right through us, past the facade, and into the truth about our intentions and the genuineness of our actions. Once we realize this, we can stop playing games, lying, and trying so hard to be something we're not. We can stop showing up like a needy kid desperate for approval (or a big piece of new business) and begin acting like normal humans.

The lines of separation between work and personal life are more blurred now than ever before. Since we are all connected, and my thoughts and actions have an impact on many others around me, I am accountable. However, I am not accountable to be perfect. I am accountable to be conscious, to be honest - with others and myself - and to live with integrity and passion.

Most individual contributors and business owners are not content with a purely transactional relationship with their work. They do care, and care deeply. Most in business care (or want to care) about what they are doing, the contribution they are making to their organization, solving problems for clients, and working as a team alongside co-workers. They want to feel proud about what they are doing and feel that their work, in some way, serves a purpose larger than just a day's wages.

Increased Commoditization and De-humanization in Professional Sales

"We are very busy. There is a lot of noise. There used to be ten mediums of advertising in our lives. Today there are hundreds of mediums for advertising. Buyers are skeptical and risk adverse. They have the Internet at their disposal. Buyers have more power than they used to have. The web is talking about your product and service. The market is alive. There is very little time to think."
— Paul Lorinczi, Business Owner

With access to more information than ever before, consumers of any product or service, especially complex ones, are feeling more in control. They shop price, compare features, negotiate the best deal, and feel empowered. In most industries, at least on the surface, supply outstrips demand. This newfound power shift drives customers to demand more from both their vendors and the whole buying experience. There are many positives, as a retail customer or business client, to having more information and control. In turn, the negative result for most organizations' sales teams is a feeling of being squeezed, pressured, and even intimidated to compete on price, give discounts, and jump through more hoops than ever to get new business. What was once a *relationship sell* is now often driven by spreadsheets and low-level personnel in charge of getting the best deal with no sense of the bigger picture. Some business verticals are feeling this more than others, but the commoditization of most products, and increasingly with services as well, is the norm more than the exception.

> *"So many contracts were going these days to the advertising firms that were selling just numbers, not creative instinct. It's like they have cut all the fat out of the business and turned everything into a numbers game. But the fat is what gives meat its taste. The leanest cuts of meat don't taste very good. You want it marbled with at least a little fat. Fat is also what gives life taste and texture."*
> — Ken Greer in *The World is Flat*, by Thomas Friedman

When defaulting to the same process for engaging prospects, the same mindset when negotiating new business, and the same buzzwords and tired business marketing language, companies are more apt to fall into this "commodity" trap. Finding a way to genuinely differentiate yourself, better communicate your value, take back control of the sales process, and get to the human elements of why clients buy, is the only way to keep yourself from getting stuck in this "commodity box." This takes an upgraded set of skills in your **Thinking, Language,** and **Process.**

My clients are business-to-business professionals with ten, twenty, thirty plus years of experience. They have seen a change in the landscape and, frankly, they don't like what they see. They tell me about losing human contact and getting caught working through email only. They are competing against multiple bids with a gatekeeper that doesn't necessarily understand (or care) about the root of their company's need and who is truly best suited to help solve their problems. Even the simplest products have differentiating factors, including the people and companies that are backing them up, servicing them, and ensuring the customer is getting their money's worth. Even in this commoditized business world, there is a difference between you and your competition. It is your job to better understand and communicate this, as well as consider a different approach to how you engage with new prospective clients to find out if you are a good fit.

> *"Everything is by email now. I am dealing with a young kid at X and he says "just email me your bid." I've never met him. Half the time he doesn't get back to me. I am not sure how to deal with him…*
> *All anyone cares about is price."*
> —Thomas Friedman, quoting an unnamed friend, in *The World is Flat*

Just getting people's time these days is a challenge. Everyone is overwhelmed with information. As John O'Keefe says in his book, *Business Beyond the Box*, we have moved from "information overload" to "information pollution." How do we know what is useful information designed to serve our best interests and what is useless noise and miscellaneous garbage? Our brains are looking for patterns to recognize, filtering information in and out while deciding if something warrants more attention, action, or deletion. We are protective of our time and space and resent being pressured, pushed, or bothered. Most people lack the capacities to deal with all of this. All the more reason a sales and business communication approach that is non-threatening, clear, and looking for up front buy-in is the only way to effectively engage with clients.

"Knowledge is different than information. Knowledge is a far bigger asset in achieving step-change results. However, more and more individuals and organizations are getting bogged down in sifting and sorting masses and masses of information. The more energy and time are spent doing this, the less are spent on building really good know-how. The organization needs to learn to bypass information to get to know-how. Having more information will not give you a sustainable competitive edge. In fact, more and more information will actually hurt rather than help. It is like salt on your food. None is too little; there is an amount that makes things just right."
— John O'Keefe, Business Beyond the Box

Your process for reaching out, communicating, and engaging with prospects is in-and-of-itself an opportunity for differentiation. Every interaction, from day one, is a chance to stand out and give your prospects a different experience than your competitors can offer. This is not necessarily about giving people more information and pretty PowerPoints, or bending over backwards to kiss their butt. It's as much about what kinds of questions you ask, how you handle their tough questions, your mindset, body language, and overall demeanor. In my work as salesperson, business owner, and coach / consultant to others, I've found what most people find refreshing and attractive is direct, honest, and *human* business communication. People don't have time for the b.s. any more. They do still want to be treated respectfully, professionally, and want measurable results. Even something as simple as finding out if a prospect is "open to" a brief conversation before launching into your "pitch" is an effective and refreshing departure from the old way of doing things (although many telemarketers still don't get this).

Business-to-business sales organizations have moved away from a structure in which multiple business units sell separately to the same customer. More often now, sales resources work together to sell many products and services to the customer with one primary point of contact. With more of a focus on integrated solutions, it is requiring a heightened level of sophistication of psychology, strategy, and communication while orchestrating a complex client engagement process. New skills, tools, and talents are needed - and not just faster laptops or neater PowerPoint presentations.

> "Society today faces more complete, urgent, and
> unpredictable circumstances than in the past, forcing us to
> "make more sophisticated decisions in less time."
> — Thomas Homer-Dixon, The Ingenuity Gap
> (As quoted in Fast Company Magazine by Lucas Conley, July 2006)

The deeper we get into the hole of being overwhelmed, the more easily we default to purely rational, logical arguments. These data-driven approaches put all of their eggs into spreadsheets, systems, and business processes. Now, there are plenty of good things about these tools, but there is a human and emotional element that many have quickly forgotten. There are a lot of important variables and leveragable opportunities that many organizations seem to be losing sight of or trying to cut out.

The typical, modern sales process (especially from the buyer's side) attempts to neutralize the human, emotional variables. This is done through the RFP process with multiple bidders, long and complex forms, and little human contact. I understand that some of this approach is efficient and necessary and can't be eliminated entirely. That being said, working to eliminate some of the perceived "inefficiencies" in the process for engaging a new vendor / partner is no guarantee that you give yourself a better chance of finding the right solution. In many cases, more robotic, data-driven approaches to engaging with a new vendor / partner can actually cause more inefficiencies. This is especially true when the wrong people are making the decisions. The ones that would most benefit from investing in a new solution are being "protected" and kept out of the process. Sellers are defaulting to the buyer's process and just going along with the program, afraid if they speak up or what I call *push back*, they will lose "the opportunity of a lifetime." Often the prospect doesn't really know what they want and doesn't know exactly how to go about getting the help they need.

The system has over-corrected and is out of balance. The days of the three martini business lunch with your sales rep are gone and replaced by a new system that goes too far in the opposite direction. We are in need of finding a middle ground that benefits all parties. Both parties in a prospective new engagement can share control, have the same information, and work as equals in an adult-to-adult interaction. No manipulation, no grovelling, no fear, no withholding information, no posturing, no b.s.

"They gather and consider far more information than is truly necessary because it makes them feel more confident — and with someone's life in the balance, they need to feel more confident. The irony, though, is that that very desire for confidence is precisely what ends up undermining the accuracy of their decision."
— Malcolm Gladwell, Blink

Sometimes we spend so much time making sure we have all the right information that we either wait too long to act or don't ever do anything at all. To help us feel confident, we cling to every morsel of marginally relevant data about a company, its people, its past performance, its vision for the future, etc. While we're gathering more of this information than we could ever use, we're often missing the most important points: the fundamental questions about what is motivating the prospect's desire for a change and what key cues will best help both parties decide whether or not you (the seller) are really the right solution to get the problem solved. You absolutely need to be informed. And I believe that you also need to stay focused and *lean* when it comes to the level of information you seek out and absorb regarding new prospects. Instead of just being focused on showing your knowledge of their company and your product / service, you must spend equal energy on the "little things" like key questions that must be asked, and ways to better control the engagement process to ensure you're a good fit.

Change Is the New Reality

With every new generation and business cycle we hear about how "times have changed," and things are more complicated and difficult than ever before. I believe things really are different now, especially regarding business and communication. New thinking and new models are required to just stay viable and in the game much less to succeed at a high level.

It is proving a necessary and valuable asset to be able to adapt and interrupt old patterns, old models, to try new things, and develop more of our capacity — both within ourselves, the talents of our people, and in our organizations. We really cannot work any HARDER. We can work differently. To act differently and have it sustain results, we have to think differently. This is hard for most humans, especially as we add age, experience, and a little gray hair. Paradoxically, it's those of us who are not the young, up and comers any more, who most need to reinvent ourselves to stay valid, productive, and demonstrate our unique value as business leaders. "Change or die" is a bold and dramatic statement that I've heard for years in the world of business. And though it seems a bit harsh, with the craze in which most companies operate, it is as, if not more relevant now than ever before.

"Americans historically have been better at adapting to the effects of this creative destruction — at embracing them, even. Capitalizing on continuous change has been the basis, in part, of our national competitive advantage."
— Keith Hammonds, Fast Company Magazine, June 2006

No job is sacred. The safety nets, pension plans, golden parachutes, and sense that larger institutions will take care of us is almost entirely dead, done, and gone. The only real job security you have is continuing to build your business networks, sharpening your communication and negotiation skills, and becoming more savvy about both your own psychology, habits, patterns, AND the psychology, habits, and patterns of others. You have a chance to influence others, negotiate, and sell every day. The better you get at these things, the more of the right clients you gain and the more financial abundance you will attract.

"The world economy is going through a genuine epochal transformation on the scale of the industrial revolution 200 years ago... The challenges are fundamentally different and deeply unfamiliar... In an information-based economy, untethered to physical assets, business models can and will change continually."
— Fortune Magazine, Investors, Does Your CEO Have What It Takes?, Geoffrey Colvin, February 2006

Big companies still have some obvious advantages inherent to their size - access to markets, capitalization, name recognition, etc. In this age of *The World is Flat*, however, the large organizations are also more vulnerable than ever. Vulnerable to quick, viral levels of competition from upstart players that "play big" - leveraging technology and a lightening quick ability to build scalable networks seemingly overnight. The more nimble, youthful, and fresh the big companies can think and appear to their customers, the more of a chance they have of staying on top. The big guys today are more scared than many of the entrepreneurial start-ups, first because they have farther to fall and second because many of their built in advantages are becoming vulnerabilities. For smaller organizations, the opportunity in this new economy to compete on a global scale with less capitalization and infrastructure is greater than ever.

"Speed. Everything is faster. Do more in less time. Consumers have more control over everything; how they shop, buy, entertain. The shift that is needed to be successful is to no longer Push things at them. Pull is what we have to do to survive and thrive in this new era."
— Roseanne Luth, Business Owner

The way business and communication are changing can work to the favor of smaller organizations with big aspirations. The challenge for younger, growing organizations is to capitalize on the advantages of appearing fresh, full of new ideas, and more progressive in how they approach their business, while also not getting categorized as too youthful, naive, or trendy. To have "legs" and sustain over time they must also show wisdom, knowledge, and experience. If they can blend this level of sophistication with the inherent advantages of being smaller, more nimble organizations, they have the opportunity to make significant impacts on the business landscape.

In the end, I believe we can all benefit from these trends. Nimbleness, entrepreneurial thinking, new ideas, continuous improvement will bring us more products at reasonable prices, new solutions to age old problems, and more abundance than ever.

"Technological advances and changing business models have diminished the importance of scale, as outsourcing, partnering, and other alliances with specialty firms have made it possible to convert fixed costs into variable ones."
— Fortune Magazine, New Rules for Winning
Betsy Morris, July 2006

The unique state of the business world today doesn't afford much margin for error. Attachment to old, outdated ideas (that at one time were the right way to do things) is causing the failure of a multitude of organizations, large and small. Sales consultant Frank Rumbauskas, Jr. speaks to this in his reference to the "creative destruction" that is a natural by-product of capitalism. This concept was first coined by Dr. Joseph A. Schumpeter, the former Austrian Minister of Finance and Harvard Business School professor. He talks about the perpetual cycle of destroying old, less-efficient business models and ideas and replacing them with new, more-efficient ones.

This feature of capitalism is inevitable and unavoidable. You have a choice to do the right things to avoid falling into this trap for yourself.

> *"There is no way to create wealth without ideas. Most new ideas are created by newcomers. So anyone who thinks the world is safe for incumbents is dead wrong."*
> — Gary Hamel, Leading the Revolution

As the solutions in business and the marketplace have changed, so too have the questions we must ask. In this time of great change, asking the right questions, of yourself, your team, your organization, and of course your prospective clients is as important as having the answers. How well are you adapting to this changing landscape? Who is pushing and challenging you? Are you insulated by people that will tell you what you want to hear? Do you have people inside and outside of your organization that are helping support and challenge you to think differently about your business, yourself, and your team?

Progressive leaders willing to invest time, energy, and money into upgrading their skills, reinventing their processes, and becoming savvier about the psychology of sales, negotiation, and business communication are differentiating themselves from the pack. In my experience in the professional community, I still see ninety-five percent of all leaders behind the curve. There is a window of opportunity for you to stand head and shoulders above your competitors with a more sophisticated approach to engaging prospective clients, a deeper understanding of your unique value, and more sustainable ways to motivate your people (and yourself) to change.

"When it comes to thriving in a hypercompetitive marketplace, "playing it safe" is no longer playing it smart. In an economy defined by overcapacity, oversupply and utter sensory overload – an economy in which everyone already has more than enough of whatever you're selling – the only way to stand out from the crowd is to stand for a truly distinctive set of ideas about where your company should be going. You can't do big things as a competitor if you're content with doing things only a little better than the competition...Mavericks do the work that matters most – the work of originality, creativity and experimentation."

— Bill Taylor, Mavericks at Work

YOUR EGO COSTS YOU TIME AND MONEY

Preview Points:

- Understanding your ego and its motivations is essential for creating sustained success.

- Forcing things and holding on too tight for too long will wear you out.

- Hearing, "no" and saying, "I don't know" won't kill you, despite what your ego will try to tell you.

"Most organizations continue to believe that the issues of productivity, efficiency, or quality control are large enough to contain a business. These, however, are characteristics more associated with machines and hierarchical systems than with groups of human beings working together. People and ideas are less easily contained, far less predictable, and infinitely more complex."
— Jerry Hirshberg, The Creative Priority

Building Your House on a Shaky Foundation

You might wonder, *"What the heck does ego have to do with sales, business communication, and negotiation?"* The real question should be, "What part of the sales process doesn't involve the ego?" The ego is the driver of everything that we're talking about in this book. It is the undercurrent behind all the key principles I have found lead to more accelerated results and sustainable change in the area of sales, sales leadership, and business growth. The ego is useful to you in some ways, and yet it is destructive in many others. Becoming more aware of when your ego is doing the talking, what it's saying, and why you default to it is an important first step. There are a number of specific situations in sales, negotiation, and business communication where your ego's compulsive reactions can cause you unnecessary stress and cost you time and money.

The ego self is built upon more of a straw hut than a brick building. Even if it appears solid and strong on the surface, it can crumble at any moment. It's always at the mercy of external influences: who's loving me; who thinks I'm great; who am I better than; am I right; am I getting validation that I'm smart, good, sexy, cool. To better understand this, try and picture the ego as a separate thing, a little creature living inside your head. It (your ego) continually struggles to stay "alive" and in control. It is constantly working to protect itself and find ways to grow and gain influence over you and over others. For those of you well versed in Looney Tunes cartoons from the 1960s and 70s, imagine a little *Tasmanian Devil* character inside your head.

Our ego's desire for and belief in its separation gets in the way of our ability to effectively communicate. If it can stay independent of any influence or power except its own, then it can control, never get hurt, and never be surprised. From this state, it's impossible to be authentically curious, detached from the outcome, and listen effectively. The ego is very inefficient in its ability to drive high-quality sustainable business growth and ideal client engagements. Your ego can power achievement, but it cannot power sustainable relationships and optimal efficiency.

> *"What happens when people attempt to change external reality without any prior change in their inner reality, their state of consciousness. They make plans without taking into account the blueprint for dysfunction that every human being carries within: the ego."*
> — Eckhart Tolle, A New Earth

Whether in the headlines or on a *VH-1 Behind the Music* story, how many tales of corporate, political, or celebrity scandals have you seen in the last few years? They are everywhere, and at the foundation of each is the ego. Its insatiable appetite for more, the compulsive desire for validation, and the blindness, denial, and sheer stupidity it causes eventually leads to the fall.

All this being said, I'm not suggesting that we all need to become egoless monks pacing peacefully in silence. But, the influence our ego has on our daily actions, good and bad, is crucial. Our culture pumps us with ego-based messages and weaves them into the fabric of our lives - "Hit the home run!", "Don't take no for an answer!", "We will stay the course at all costs!" You don't have to sell your expensive foreign car, move out of your nice house, or stop going to the mall. There's nothing wrong with having lots of money and enjoying nice things. The process of purchasing things, decorating a house, or driving a nice car can be stimulating, interesting, and fun. I love the freedom and flexibility that money can bring. Where we get in trouble, though, is when we get overly identified with these things, too attached to them, and afraid we might lose them. I see this happen too often in the process of selling yourself to new clients and closing the "big deal."

When driven by compulsions that we don't understand or control, we are building our success on a very shaky foundation. How many people have you seen hit it big, make lots of money, and ride high on the hog when you just knew in your gut that something was out of balance? There are thousands of examples of success built on the unstable foundation of a compulsion to be good enough or smart enough and a fear of losing it all once we get to the top. I was talking to a prospective new client recently who had made and lost $10 million over the course of five years. Thanks to a personality that was compulsively driven to please everyone, he made bad decisions and gave all his money away, to the wrong people and the wrong deals. He is now beginning to sort out the wreckage of his life and start over, both personally and professionally. The first step is understanding what happened, and taking responsibility for his part in it, and not just playing the victim of circumstance card.

> *"The world of ego is brittle, fragile, and insecure; it never feels really safe, and it has no lasting worth. The ego's world dies. More often than not, it self-destructs."*
> — Stuart Wilde, Silent Power

Last year, I watched the documentary film, *Enron: The Smartest Guys in the Room*. We all know the basic story of Enron, of course. It's a tragic tale about greed and misguided intentions. As easy as it is to categorize the Enron leadership and their supporters as inherently evil, we all have similar elements in our make-up. We all have some capacity deep within us to get scared, become attached, mislead, lie, and find ways to justify our behavior. The deeper in we get, the more we are afraid to come clean. As the white lies become real lies and we get afraid of the repercussions, it gets harder and harder to just tell the truth.

One of my favorite terms to use when working with business leaders and professionals responsible for developing new business is "thoughtful, radical honesty." The more direct and transparent you are right up front with your prospective clients and business partners, the better chance you have for long-lasting, sustainable relationships. You set the tone with honest and clear agreements and expectations. Too often, this is not happening. Most people are afraid of scaring prospects away. They are afraid of what might happen if you tell them everything about who you are and what they can and should not expect from doing business with you. What you are most afraid of someone finding out, always gets found out eventually. The inevitable just gets put off for a few days, weeks, or months. And the longer a relationship goes built upon an unstable foundation, the uglier the break-up.

The ego takes EVERYTHING personally

When people don't call back. It amazes me what a hold the ego has on us. I was speaking with a past client not too long ago who is a very successful entrepreneur. He has made lots of money and accomplished more than ninety-nine percent of the world. He was still out there selling and looking to generate more new business. He doesn't do this because he needs the money actually, but because he loves a challenge and wants to stay engaged in life and work. The interesting thing is that for such a seasoned, wise, and successful man, there was still part of his ego that had a grip on him. He said the one thing that was most impactful about our work together was that I helped him take "no" less personally. He learned to move on, let go, and not be so offended by a "no" response. His ego had an expectation of how people are supposed to act and react and when things didn't go his way, the ego would throw a fit. Gradually he gained control and now can move on to other opportunities much more easily, although he still needs a little reminder every now and then.

When someone doesn't call you back, you can't force a different outcome. You can give yourself the best possible chance to get a response and move things forward, but in the end, you cannot control the other person's behavior, level of openness, honesty, etc. Your desire to do so will cause you a lot of frustration. Focus on what you can control, learn to do that more effectively, and learn to let go of what you can't control.

*"Self-importance requires that one spend most of one's life
offended by something or someone."*
— Carlos Castaneda

The ego is terrified of being invisible and un-acknowl-edged. Truth is, everyone wants to be seen, heard, understood, loved, and appreciated. There is nothing wrong with that. It becomes a problem when you are compulsively looking for that outside of yourself. You can't get from others what you're not giving to and receiving from within yourself. If you are selling, negotiating, and trying to grow your business from a place of not-good enough, you will show up that way and allow others to discount you and treat you poorly. You will chase prospective clients and potential business partnerships around who are not seeing or appreciating your value and wonder why they are not "getting it." I know none of us want to admit it, but we all do it, at some level, or have been guilty of getting caught in this trap in a personal relationship, at the office, or with a new business prospect. This aspect of the ego can sabotage and compromise your position of strength and opportunity to negotiate a solution or sale that is truly best for all parties. Any neediness, however subtle, compromises you.

That being said, this is where an *over-correction* often occurs. I see people take this to the other extreme where they act as if they don't need anyone, don't care about the business, and are "ultra-detached." Sometimes, to settle into a new way of being and doing things, there is some natural over-correction that takes place. The key here is to know that this may happen and to try and be aware of it, correcting again to a more centered position. It's ok to care. It's NOT ok to completely *not care.* Active engagement, with curiosity, focus, and sincerity is essential, coupled with a healthy level of detachment from needing / wanting desperately for a particular outcome to occur.

In new business prospecting, you are spending lots of time trying to get people to agree to talk to you and to share the truth about their business challenges and opportunities. When being driven by your ego's desire to be seen and validated at any cost, you find yourself trying to convince people that don't really see and appreciate your value. They either get it or they don't. They are either open or they are not. This is either because it's not the right time or you are truly not the right fit, or some combination. Or, because you didn't effectively communicate you weren't able to get them to open up and give you the whole truth. No matter what the reason, at some point, people are ready and open and see your value or at least are open to actively engage and talk to you in your client engagement process, or they are not. Simple as that.

Ego Wants You to See Yourself as Separate

The ego's sole purpose is to uphold the illusion that you alone are at the center of all situations and separate from other people. The ego helps construct a sense of self able to cope and keep it "together" in a complex world, keeping you from falling apart during stressful situations. Edward Edinger, M.D. speaks of our desire to protect ourselves that drives our creation of a *persona* (Latin word for an ancient "actor's mask"). This is our public face. When you under-identify (i.e.: feel too exposed or sensitive) or over-identify (i.e.: get too rigid or defensive) with this persona, you can get disconnected from what is real. It is these two extremes that cause most of the ineffectiveness in business situations, especially high-level sales and negotiations. If you are too removed from the human elements in a negotiation, you are missing a tremendous opportunity to get what you want (and to help others get what they want). When you are disconnected, it's much easier to manipulate, intimidate, withhold information, and even lie. If you're overly sensitive, you will be ripe for being swayed by others' bullying, intimidation, and lies. There is an optimal *middle place* that is neither too disconnected nor too sensitive that is at the heart of the approach that I suggest is most effective.

> *"Your ability to "will yourself" toward whatever you desire.*
> *Pit bull determination. Having a strong will and being filled with resolve*
> *to accomplish inner goals is asking ego to be the guiding force in your life.*
> *I will do this thing, I will never be stupid, I will never give up. Your will*
> *power is so much less effective than your imagination."*
> — Wayne Dyer, The Power of Intention

Resisting "What Is"

Our emotions are reactions driven by the ego. The ego establishes rules. When things go according to those rules, then everything is great (happy). When the ego's idea of what is supposed to be happening is contradicted by the reality of what is actually happening, things are bad (unhappy). The more ideas you have about how things are supposed to be and what is supposed to happen next, the more apt you are to be disappointed. Unless, that is, you can find a way to control every element of your life and everyone else's around you. Sounds tiring just thinking about it, doesn't it? When you make a conscious decision NOT to react to the ego of others, particularly in business negotiation and high stakes sales situations, you will often be able to bring out more rational and even-keeled responses. As you get better at bringing this out in others, you have more of a chance of finding out what they really need and being able to help them with their problem or opportunity. You can only bring out the rational, human, even-keeled reactions in others if you yourself are conscious, aware, and thinking, talking, and acting in these same ways. You yourself must model the mindset and behavior that you want to see from others.

In addition to separation and desire, the ego's stubborn resistance to reality can frustrate you and waste a lot of time and energy. Our inflexible idea of what is "supposed to be happening" at each moment is in our minds all the time (i.e.: my coffee is supposed to hot, my food is supposed to come quickly, there's no reason that traffic should be slowing down just because it's raining a little bit). When things don't go our way, we often can revert back to behaviors we learned as young children.

Notice when your mind throws a mini-tantrum because someone won't call you back or just doesn't seem to "get" why they need you to help solve their problems. Often, these emotional reactions of the mind cause us to do crazy things — think of the *"Can't let it go, ex-boyfriend (or girlfriend)"* that keeps calling and sending gifts. Most everyone has either had someone like this or has been this person once in their life. Sometimes we have to give it up, surrender, and move on - at least for the time being. I know it's not in fashion these days to say this, and there's a lot of praise for people who never give up and stay the course no matter what. I'm not suggesting you not be committed to succeeding. You can't force behaviors on other people, though. It's a fine line, but at some point, persistence becomes annoyance. No one wants to be "that guy" that just couldn't give it up and made a fool of himself with the girl that was out of his league. Sometimes it pays off, at least that's what we see in the movies. More often than not, it's a HUGE waste of time and energy, not to mention a blow to one's self image.

Don't be desperate. Don't try to intimidate, manipulate, or force. Be savvy about getting people to open up and engage with you. But if it's not going anywhere, bail out. Tell them, without annoyance or emotion, that you're going away. Then do exactly that: go away, move on. It may not be forever, but at least for now find another opportunity to work on. Remember that right timing and having a good fit are not things you can force even though the ego-voice in your head will try and tell you otherwise.

Ego Puts Everything in a Box

The ego will also put people and situations in boxes as quickly as possible. It will tell us things are good or bad, smart or dumb, useful or useless, safe or unsafe. The ego's job, or so it believes, is to keep us safe from harm, to minimize pain, and maximize pleasure. It's constantly, vigilantly scanning for a connection to "tags" in our memories trying to ensure we repeat good experiences and don't recreate bad ones. This can be useful when sizing up situations to figure out how you're going to react, determining how much time and energy you're going to allot, and what your approach will be. Some of this is fueled by gut-level intuition and the lens through which you see the world and can be useful to help you sort out the complex demands on your time and energy on a daily basis. In sales and negotiation, we can sometimes rush too quickly to label a situation as a "big opportunity" or a "worthless dead end." Our intuition can serve us well and can also fail miserably if our emotions lead us to follow a big prospect that from the beginning was probably a dead end. It can also lead us to too quickly rule out a prospect that might in the end be a great fit.

One way to help is to have a process for key situations. To have a process for each step, guiding principle, and mindset filter you create for an RFP, new business opportunity, first meeting with a prospect, etc. Don't forget your prospect is also putting you in a "box" based on their experiences. This presents an opportunity for you to do or say something to attempt to get yourself out of "the box" they've placed you in. This can be a new question, having a different kind of conversation, or using a more straightforward and honest manner.

The Ego Compares: Puts you in a One-Down or One-Up Position

The ego lives through comparison. It looks at others and puts one's self in either a one-down *not good enough* position or a one-up *better than* position. It is very impressed by others. It loves to worship the likes of Mark Cuban, Bill Gates, and Steve Jobs, to name a few. The more we indulge in the ego-admiring, wanting to be like them, and seeing others as *better than* or *different from* us, the further away we get from our own path of self realization and what true success looks like on our life's path. While some of this *wanting* can be a driver, it is more often a distraction. The most concerning part about this for me is that it pulls most of us away from being authentic; thoughtfully, radically honest and fully human in professional situations. Many of the thinking, language, and process suggestions in the following chapters, if followed, will help alleviate this.

As much as we try to put ourselves in an equal position in high-stakes sales and negotiation when we are calling higher in an organization (i.e.: the CEO's office instead of the purchasing manager) or working on the "biggest deal of our life," we can often get nervous and put those we're meeting with on a pedestal as better or more powerful than us. The ability to NOT do this is a learned discipline and much easier said than done. You must first be aware of this fear before you can just move through it and make the call. There is no better way to get more comfortable with this than through the repetition of practice. You have to re-train your brain and remind yourself that this person across the table, no matter what his title, size of his paycheck, or celebrity status, is a human being just like you and thus not any better than you.

Ego Argues and Tries to Convince

It takes a high level of awareness and discipline not to argue. The ego LOVES to argue and debate. It takes everything very seriously. This all comes from a wicked combination of arrogance and insecurity. Notice when you are arguing or working hard to persuade someone to see your position — especially when you are in a selling or negotiating situation. Your preaching and working hard to "get them to get it" has much less influence on their final decision than your ego would ever like to know or let you believe. Stop trying so hard.

When selling and negotiating there is often a natural gravitation towards wanting to be right, be validated, and win. If someone doesn't see things your way and doesn't see your value, the ego gets triggered. This can show up as getting pissed and, in schoolyard talk, wanting to "take your ball and go home." It can show up as a desperate and compulsive need to convince others to "get it." There is nothing that strengthens the ego more than **being right**. Being right is identification with a mental position: a perspective, an opinion, a judgment, or a story. For you to be right, of course, you need someone else to be wrong which gives your ego a stronger sense of identity.

"Force is the universal substitute for truth... the need to control others stems from lack of power, just as vanity stems from a lack of self-esteem."
— David Hawkins, Power vs. Force

A client of mine shared a story about coaching one of his co-workers. This co-worker was attempting to generate new business from a large account and was distraught after meeting with them. He felt strongly that he lost the opportunity to move to the next step and get invited back because, "I didn't do a good job convincing them of our value." My client, with some new perspective on what it meant to "sell," suggested to him that maybe it's not his job to convince anyone of anything. He reminded him that it is his job to demonstrate the company's value as it relates to the prospect's current challenges and/or opportunities, to facilitate an open and honest discussion, and then the correct decision becomes self-evident. You either have a fit, or you don't. We all are making choices every day about what we are open to, what we want more of, less of, how we spend our time, who we align ourselves with, etc. This prospect made a choice. There wasn't any level of convincing, trying harder, selling harder, giving more information, creating cooler PowerPoints, or doing a more engaging dog and pony show that could make a difference.

Your ego thinks you should be spending your time and energy convincing people how great you are, showing how smart you are, assuming you know what's best for your prospects, and forcing your agenda and needs into the situation. At some level this can work to make you successful. It's just a lot of effort and takes a lot of extra energy. And none of it is really sustainable. You have to keep re-establishing new relationships with new clients where many of the old clients quickly fell away. You can convince, compel, and seduce people to do business with you. It's just more efficient and profitable in the short and long term if you can get THEM to convince YOU why it makes sense to do business together.

I received this note from a client who is a manager, salesperson and professional services expert the other day. She talks about this need to get others to "get it" better than I can...

"You taught me to be strong at letting go, especially with potential clients that aren't a good fit for me, are not what I'm looking for more of, are a lot of work, don't really get it and are not rewarding to help. They are good people I'm sure, but for what I'm trying to build are a waste of my time and energy...My assistant and I coined a phrase "Stop

71

bending over backwards trying to go forward". When it's too hard, too forced, too much work, even in the name of making more money or adding a client, it's often counterproductive, yet there is a compulsive tug within that says I must help this person in front of me, I am obligated to do all I can to help them, take them on, work hard to get them to get it. I've realized that voice does not serve me and my goals, and truthfully doesn't serve the prospective client either. So, when this happens, I call it out — to myself, and with the help of my assistant. And I push back. Push back on this thought, push back respectfully on the prospective client. At this point, they have to convince me why it makes sense to work together or I tell them maybe it doesn't make sense to move forward. Half the time, they go away, which at first was scary, but now is great, because I have room to work on more ideal clients and attracting a new prospect that is a better fit for me. Half the time they respond, shifting their attitude and actions, shaping into more of the client I need them to be to feel good about investing my time and energy in them. Either way, I win."

— Deborah Lawrence, Financial Advisor

Ego Hates "I don't know"

The ego does not want you to say certain things during a negotiation or business relationship. Most of the ideas I am offering to you are things that your ego is afraid of. Such as, "I don't have any idea if I can help you" and "I'm not sure what we do is right for you." These statements will draw others to you instead of you chasing and convincing them.

Right off the bat, when a new client asks questions like, "Why should I hire you?" or "Why do you think this project should be yours?", this is a both trap and an opportunity. It is designed to put you on the defensive and make you perform, or to "dance," as I call it. If you play this game, both your ego and your client's will jockey for position. There is no authentic connection and you will lose most opportunities to uncover the real issues and genuinely find out if you can help.

The key here is neutralizing the egos. The first pattern interrupt that is essential for these kinds of situations is to NOT answer their questions directly, because they are not productive questions. If you answer them at the surface level they will not really give your prospect the kind of meaningful information they need to make a decision. Even though the prospect thinks they are the right questions, they can be a trap that gets you caught sounding like everyone else. And if you start answering them, you will immediately lose control and will have little chance of regaining it. The first answer starts with, "*I don't know.*" Your ego hates this. Your ego thinks their ego is going to believe that you are weak and unsure. To the ego this is an immediate nail in the coffin – dead man walking! This kind of approach can feel very counterintuitive to our traditional desire to convince, persuade, or impress someone. Your first obligation is to be radically honest. Truth is, you do not know why they should hire you, because you don't know enough yet about their problems, concerns, opportunities, the people who care, who makes the decisions, the levels of urgency, and what they are and are not open to. Don't pretend that you do.

What you can give them is an idea of why your clients hire you and what they were struggling with and looking to achieve when you first engaged. You must also establish up front that, to best use their time and yours, you need to ask some questions. This conversation HAS to be a two-way, adult exchange. Do not get caught in what I call being the "dancing monkey." The dancing monkey is there to perform on command, to submit to its master, and do anything to please others as long as it gets a few treats and some momentary admiration. If you default to your new prospect's process and just follow along at every step of the way, you reinforce that they are the ones in control with all the leverage. The key is having a process that allows you to negotiate from a position of equality, or what I call "All-Even," without seeming like you're being overly controlling or difficult. We will talk more later about the detailed elements that need to come together to allow you to do this.

"No" Needs to Be Completely OK

At every step along the way of your client engagement process, there are always two possible outcomes — "Yes, let's move forward to the next step," or, "No, we're done." Both parties are making this choice at each step in the process. Especially at the beginning of a client engagement process with a new prospect, letting them know that "no" is a completely acceptable answer is essential. The challenge here is that you have to mean it.

Your ego is going to hate this. The ego thinks you're letting the prospect off the hook and being *soft* if you give them an out. Despite what the ego will tell you, this is not the case. People always have this choice; we just don't talk about it because we're afraid to hear "no." By acknowledging the obvious here (which most of your competition is not doing), you have a chance to build more trust quickly. The more trust, the more truth, and more of a chance to find out if there is enough reason to do business together. The more "ok" we can get with a "no," the more efficient and effective we'll be with our sales process and the use of our time and energy. This high intent, confidence, and honesty is refreshing to most. I promise that you'll win more new business than you'll lose with this mindset and overall approach.

Q: What do you find salespeople, business professionals most struggle with today?
A: "Being themselves and dealing with the fear of letting go of ego —
for many it is probably akin to jumping out of a plane without a parachute."
— Mark Sandler, Vice President Sales / Client Services

In summary, here are a few things to keep in mind. Seek to better understand how these show up in your day-to-day actions, how you think they help you, and how they might also hold you back. Clients often ask me to help them get rid of these ego-driven, compulsive thoughts and actions. To create sustained change, you cannot alter these habits, patterns, and reactions overnight. You can't just wake up tomorrow and "get rid of them." You can start by being more conscious and aware of when your ego voice shows up, and how it specifically affects your approach to negotiation, dealing with difficult situations, and developing new business. These reminders are designed to help you close more new business, get more of what you want from others on your team with less stress, and to be more in control of your results.

Key Reminders:

- Detach. This does not mean don't care. It does suggest being more aware of and working to eliminate actions and thoughts that are driven by fear.

- Learn from your mistakes, but don't dwell on them and beat yourself up. Give yourself a break and remember, "It's all learning." Be curious and interested in what you did, thought, what happened, what worked, what didn't work, and how to do it better next time.

- In sales, negotiation, and relevant life situations, let people (prospects/clients/etc.) know right up front that "no" is a completely acceptable answer. And mean it. At the same time, notice your ego's fear of giving people an "out."

- When things don't seem to be going as you envisioned, notice resistance, anger, and thoughts about the way things "should be," what's "not fair," or any other victim-inspired thoughts about what's happening to you. This is the ego throwing a temper tantrum. Only when you are consciously aware of this in the moment can you then make a choice to let it go. Awareness is the antidote that gives you the best chance to make a different, more productive choice around how you spend your energy.

- Risk not knowing — this creates the space for your prospect to come to you, give you more information, and be equally motivated to engage. When you talk too much and claim to have all the answers about everything, you will often scare new people away.

- Notice when you are chasing and reacting, or feeling scattered and anxious. Relax, slow down, talk less.

- Be normal. Be yourself. You are a valuable person. You don't need to try too hard, force things, or push to impress.

ATTACHMENT
TO AMBIGUITY

Preview Points:

- Many in sales fear clarity and are unconsciously ambiguous.
- We waste energy "hoping" things are going to happen, unwilling to move on.
- Fear of "no" costs you a lot of time and even more money.

Ambiguity: Uncertainty of meaning or intention. An unclear, indefinite, word, expression, meaning.

One of my main tasks is to help you eliminate, or at least minimize, ambiguity. I have witnessed an interesting and odd tick in most people's mental makeup that allows them to tolerate and even create ambiguity in their lives. In sales and all new business development efforts, ambiguity can cost you significant amounts of time and money.

Many business and sales professionals have told me that, at times, they actually like ambiguity and fear clarity. If they don't have a "no" then they are still in the game and can keep doing things to persuade someone to buy. While this is true at some level, it's incredibly inefficient thinking. NOT taking the steps needed to get the truth about what's going on for your prospect and finding out what they are and are not open to is a recipe for wasted time and effort. As an entrepreneur, sales professional, or anyone else responsible for developing new business, your primary job is to get the truth from your prospects and clients as early in the process as possible. Truth is ambiguity's *kryptonite*.

Most people who sell are deathly afraid of "no." I'm telling you, "no" is your friend. I know that sounds crazy, especially when you have been taught to "get to yes" your entire career. If the answer is "no" then you should want to know that. You don't want to be the last one to learn a client isn't interested in your proposal after you've invested a huge amount of time and effort. The more quickly and clearly you can categorize you prospects (and clients), the more efficient you can be with where you spend your time and energy. Of course, you should always put your best foot forward and give yourself the best chance of getting a yes. I am interested in providing you with new thinking, language, and process-related tools to hear "yes" more often, from the right kinds of clients. In order to get there, you must also be willing to hear "no" and to move on.

This approach is about how to more efficiently attract the right people into your new client engagement process and more quickly move the wrong prospects out. If now is not the time or they are not a good fit, you must learn to move on, the sooner the better. This doesn't mean you can't ever talk to them again or reach out at some point in the future. In the spirit of minimizing ambiguity, the quicker and more effectively we uncover if you have a good fit, the better for all involved. Attachment to ambiguity and fear of truth and clarity is a thinking issue (fear of hearing no), a language issue (lack of compelling language about your value), and a process issue (no control of or vision for next steps). All of these tools are designed to assist you or your team to be clearer, more efficient with your time and energy spent in business development activities.

I would like you to consider that ambiguity is an illness - a nasty virus that you want to avoid like the plague. Become intolerant of it, even repulsed by it. Get vigilant about eliminating ambiguity from your business development process. Examine your tolerance for ambiguity, especially as it relates to your prospecting pipeline and new opportunities with existing clients. Are you moving things effectively *into* and *out of* your process? Are you holding on to things that are probably already dead, but you find yourself still pushing or stalling because you're afraid of hearing *no*? What is the cost of ambiguity to you in your business development efforts? Is this primarily a thinking issue, a language issue, or a process issue for you and your team? How do you contribute to things being left ambiguous? What can you do to be more specific and clearer to ensure you are moving things forward or letting things go?

> *"A common human and organizational habit is to dream vaguely and dread precisely. We are vague about the possibilities of future achievement; but we are precise about all the barriers, the negatives, the reasons it can't be done. These come quickly and easily to mind. Dream as precisely as you can. Dread as vaguely as you can."*
> — John O'Keefe, Business Beyond the Box

As you read the sections that follow, be aware how ambiguity can be created in your new client engagement process and overall business communication. What's your part in that? How might you be clearer about next steps, agreements, and how you communicate? Look at where you get uncomfortable and even have some fear of clarity, asking questions, or suggesting steps that would eliminate ambiguity. Remember that even if your rational mind says, *"Well of course I want clarity and would like to eliminate ambiguous situations and outcomes,"* there is another part of your mind that actually likes things not being clear.

There are ways to facilitate a process that helps both you and your prospect get clear about whether or not you can help them, if they have a problem worth solving, if you talking to the right person, etc. Keep in mind they are struggling with the same things you are. They often have no idea what they are doing, what they really need, and what the next step is. Your approach, if you're selling with integrity, is designed to help your prospect get clear about what they need, who else has a stake in getting their problem solved, and who is going to best be able to help them.

It's fine to be positive, but don't be naive and overly hopeful. As humans, we have quite a capacity for self-deception. It often seems in our best interest to be positive and hopeful. There has to be a balance. Just hoping something is going to happen does not get it done. Hanging on to things too long, with false hope, or unwarranted positivity is a complete waste of the valuable space in your mind. The better you can get at identifying these things inside of you and within your sales process, the more efficient, wealthy, and happy you will be.

Key Reminders:

- Notice hoping, being overly and unrealistically optimistic, holding on.
- Remember that *"Hope is not a strategy."* (Phrase comes from Rick Page's book *Hope is not a strategy, Six Keys to Winning the Complex Sale*)
- Remember that nothing is as great as you think it's going to be, and nothing is as bad as you think it will be. Notice that pendulum swing in your emotions and in your mind. The reality almost always lies somewhere in the middle.
- As humans, we are very tolerant of and used to anxiety and frustration. Sustained happiness and ease is very difficult for most people.

UNDERSTANDING AND COMMUNICATING YOUR UNIQUE VALUE

Preview Points:

- At a deep and meaningful level, we don't understand our unique value, personally, professionally, or organizationally.
- It's impossible to attract ideal, "life changing" clients with empty buzzwords and corporate jargon.
- You must understand why your clients buy from you, in their words, and be able to succinctly communicate this off the top of your head at all times.

"Few... have grasped the full implications of their creative capabilities, restricting their application to what they make without seeing their significance to how they do it and who they are."
—Jerry Hirshberg, The Creative Priority

In my conversations with professionals responsible for growing their business I am consistently amazed that they underestimate and fail to understand their unique value. When an organization or individual is not growing fast enough and wants to attract more of the right kinds of new business, I always start at the foundation of how they talk about their value. The most successful people are clear and concise about what they do best and why it is their clients pay a premium for their products or services. In a group workshop or private session I will ask,

"When you are communicating with a prospect, or referral source, how do you talk about what you do, your value?"

> *Q: What do you find salespeople, business professionals most struggle with today?*
> *A: "Understanding the value of the service / product they offer.*
> *Believing in the value of their time as well as their prospect's."*
> — Nahme Chokeir, Vice President Client Services

I typically give the group a couple minutes to write down a few notes and then ask them to share. The responses most often include words and phrases like...

- World class
- Competitive price
- Full Service
- Passion
- Customer is King
- Innovation
- Strategic
- Out of the Box
- Customer focused
- Cutting Edge
- Quality
- Exceed Expectations
- Market Leader
- Value-Added
- Full-Service

Do any of these sound familiar? Do they appear in your presentations, on your website, or in your language when writing or talking with prospects? Ask yourself, "What do these words mean?" "What am I really trying to say here?" "What is it about our value that is most important to convey that describes who we are, how we think, what kind of work we do, etc?" Get yourself and your team on *buzzword alert*.

Below are five examples I found with a five minute search on the Internet. I'm sure you have seen some pretty bad examples yourself. If you want to share some especially poor ones with us visit www.perficency.com/bad-value-statements.

(Company names have been changed to avoid complete embarrassment)

"Our success is predicated on our ability to integrate our functional expertise in client services with our profound methodologies and industry experience. Our approach and process is complex and cohesive but the end results are simple. We gain market share for our clients, increase revenue and deliver substantial ROI on every engagement."

"Bingham Associates offerings and our depth of experience reflect a commitment to improving performance. We offer a broad range of consulting services, behavioral and process skill models, and development experts with extensive backgrounds in designing solutions that support your strategies for growth."

"Elite Management Systems is the premier provider of industry information systems. We support and sell the industry's most comprehensive suite of software."

"The stability of AMS solutions is legendary. We are supported by a dedicated group of well qualified people."

"Advantis Healthcare provides society with superior products and services by developing innovations and solutions that improve the quality of life and satisfy customer needs, and to provide employees with meaningful work and advancement opportunities, and investors with a superior rate of return."

Blah, Blah, Boring. What's really different or unique about what you do? Often the best way to speak to this is to talk about why your clients hired you — what was going on for them in their business situation, what kinds of challenges they were facing or opportunities they were looking to capitalize on, what were they open to, and how did you help them change?

*"I think most in business, and sales in particular struggle to convey
the value of their company that differentiates them from everyone else.
Everyone wants to say we will make you more efficient, save you money,
do quality work, etc. Who does not say that?"*
— *Brandon Jeffress, National Account Manager*

---

*"Your company value is led first by
the value you have in yourself and
your unique gifts and talents."*

When working on helping someone better understand and communicate their value, one question I ask is, "What have your clients told you about why they bought / buy from you?" The answer most always is, "Well, we think it's because..." or "They buy from us because..." Then I'll repeat the question: "What have your clients TOLD YOU about why they bought from you continue to come back, and stay engaged with you?"

If you haven't asked, ask them. It can be enlightening. Why don't you ask? Is it because you might think it's rude or are afraid of the answer? What is most uncomfortable about the idea of doing this for you?

Q: Why don't you feel comfortable asking your clients
   why they do business with you?

A: *"I'm afraid to ask—I'm just happy to have the business."*

A: *"I'm afraid they will say that everyone is the same,
   us included."*

It is important to note that there will be times that a client gets caught off guard by these questions or even scared to have a truly honest conversation. They can easily brush this off and not give it any meaningful thought. Don't take this personally. Some of your clients will give you insightful, thoughtful, and valuable feedback, though. It will be worth the effort.

Concentrate on your value. Think about it, talk about it, and write about it. More than probably ever before, your prospects are overwhelmed and trying to quickly figure out if you are someone they should give any time to. It is your

"The better we can understand and connect the things that are most effortless for us and meaningful for others, the more sustainably we can grow."

job to help them get a quick and meaningful understanding of who you are, what you do, and why people hire you in order to make a more informed decision about engaging in further conversation or not.

"John is a close friend of mine who owns an advertising agency in New York City. We sat down for coffee the other day with my intent of telling him about my new business endeavor and to see if he knew of anyone I should talk to. I started asking him about his business, their challenges and where he wanted to go. I asked him what they brought to the table that other agencies don't - what differentiates them, why people buy from them. The most unbelievable thing was he couldn't answer any of those questions. He's the owner of the agency that's been open for 5 years. He is scared, attached and just looking to survive. These issues are real."
— Andrew Bogdan, Business Development Consultant

The voices, perceptions, and assumptions you have swirling around in your head are an important part of the value equation. If you are unsure of your value, then you can't communicate it clearly to your clients and they won't be able to get a clear sense of your value. Quick questions to ask yourself in the context of the work you do with your clients:

- What is your unique value?
- What do clients / co-workers tell you they most appreciate about you, the work you do, and how you go about it?
- In your role with clients, what strengths do you bring that are most relevant and useful to maintaining and growing the business?
- In your professional role what comes most naturally to you?
- In what situations, general or specific, have you experienced discounting your unique value?

Framing Your Value in the Context of Why Your Clients Hire You

Example 1: Technology Consulting Company

Things our clients are looking for when they hire us:

- They want to do more than their current tools will allow — they can't process complex data. We solve the technical challenges with an understanding that the solution has to be simple enough for their staff to use in the future.
- They won a new project and need a team to implement / develop / support the project (usually a government customer) and think we will be successful in completing the job/solving the hard problems.
- To provide staff consultants that are either smarter or work harder (or both) than their internal resources.

Example 2: Professional Services Organization

Why clients hire us. What they are looking for that we do a good job of providing:

- They are at a critical point in their business and life (i.e.: business is changing direction, looking to take their business to the next level, facing retirement).
- Have a desire to reach new levels of profitability and growth.
- Looking for validation/confirmation that they are on the right path.
- They don't have people around them that will tell them the hard truth.
- They want a partner that will help to minimize surprises.
- Provide a sense of control and stability in time of transition and growth.
- They need more input and information to make an important business decision — it's outside their realm of expertise.
- Responsiveness — someone who will return calls immediately, follow up in timely manner, and make them feel important.

If you notice, the two lists above have framed each company's value in the context of what the prospect / client is dealing with and what they are looking for. This is a fundamental shift from jumping into telling people how many years you've been in business, assets under management, or how many offices you have around the globe. In the end, people don't care about those things. Break your value down in meaningful terms, in the context of what your clients might be going through and can relate to. In order to create this approach, look at your current clients and why they hired you. What was going on for them that caused them to change what they were doing and who they were working with? What did you offer them that compelled them to sign up with you as opposed to your various competitors? Below are some more specific suggestions of how you can frame YOUR value in your PROSPECT'S WORLD.

Pain-Opportunity-Open To

I find most individuals and organizations don't fully understand, believe in, or effectively communicate their value. Your value in and of itself is meaningless, unless connected to a pain or an opportunity for your client faces. There are also things that they must be open to in order for there to be any reason to move forward. On a personal level, as all organizational value gets filtered through the individual, how you see yourself is an equally important issue.

Why do your clients choose to work with you?

Audience: Who do you sell to? What specifically describes their business (*i.e.: industry vertical, revenue, geography, etc.*)?

Pain: What kind of pain are your prospects in when they hire you? What are they struggling with? What's not working for them?

Opportunity: What are your prospects looking to achieve when they turn to you? What kind of opportunities are they looking to capitalize on?

Open to: What must they be open to if they are going to be a good fit for doing business with you? What do they have to be willing to *do, think, accept, and consider* in order to be a legitimate prospect?

If there is one element from the above list that most every-one misses on this subject, it is the phrase **"open to."** It is the least used and the most important way to frame both your value and why people buy from you —in your internal process as well as language used to communicate to clients via the web, emails, or spoken word. What happens is that you can find people that have pain or opportunities that relate to what you do, but that doesn't necessarily translate to them being open (i.e.: *open to...* change, talking, trying you out, giving you nec-essary information, letting you talk to decision makers, etc.). Here is one example from a client of mine:

When people hire us, they need to be open to:
- Sharing their concerns and problems
- Listening
- New ideas
- Change and changing their thinking
- Hard truths
- New levels of planning and discipline
- Risk
- Paying ("significant fees") for advice
- Changing their current relationship

Ask yourself again, "What do my prospects have to be "open to" in order for us to move forward in our exploratory process and have the best chance for an optimally productive working relationship?" There are things they have to be open to, and ways they must think and act that are going to make them a good fit for you, or not. Be bold and clear about this up front in your prospecting conversations, in your written communications, and presentations. You will waste less time working with bad prospects and differentiate yourself from the competition that will all sound the same.

I imagine you may have been through some version of this exercise before. That being said, I see many well meaning, smart professionals forgetting the basics. Getting back to some simple "blocking and tackling" can help re-energize and re-focus your efforts to more quickly attract the right kinds of new clients.

I hesitate to provide too many examples in this section because the answers can be very personal and industry specific. There is no right or wrong way to do this. One of my clients answered the questions about why people hire them this way.

What are our prospective clients struggling with?

- Wasted time and money.
- Need quick turn around.
- Having trouble finishing project.
- Dealing with a downsized team. They need help — lack time, resources, and energy.
- Project they won is not in their core competency.
- They want to look good to their boss — worried about their job.

What is the opportunity that we are helping our prospective clients achieve?

- Help them win more new business from high profile key accounts.
- Help them better understand what they want and need (i.e.: sometimes they don't know).
- Can make their lives easier.

- Meet deadlines.
- Help them with direction, vision.
- Take a piece of work off their plate.

What do our prospective clients need to be open to?

- Having a conversation.
- New partnerships.
- Taking a risk around trusting that we are going to come through for them.
- Being challenged.
- Sharing responsibility.
- Meeting.

Take some time to work through this exercise and discuss it with your team. Find ways to talk about your value in more compelling, human, and tangible ways. Ask some of your best clients to help you with this process. They know you and your company as well as anyone, even yourself. Use these ideas and frameworks to re-think the language you use and how you communicate what you do and who you do it for. Instead of talking about your value and how great you are *in a vacuum*, talk about it in the context of why your clients buy from you and what kinds of things they are dealing with, looking for, and open to that led them to be a good fit. From this place your client can decide what, if anything, is relevant to their situation. Make it easy on yourself; stop selling and pushing and performing.

One final thought to end this section is to consider integrating your **observations and philosophies** into your prospecting conversations and presentations. You have been working in this field for a while now, I assume, and you have developed certain "observations" — about people, about the marketplace, about what you see works well and what doesn't, etc. Remember that your unique perspective has value. It lets a client see how you think and what you believe, which in the end, should attract more of the right kinds of clients and projects. Sometimes in business, we leave this part out, or get afraid to share our observations. I believe sharing them makes you seem thoughtful, competent, and intelligent without being boastful. These observations you have made then drive the operating philosophies for how you do business. This is one more way to stand out as genuinely unique and compelling, without having to "sell" and "boast." The more specific, meaningful information you share with new prospects about why people hire you, how you see things, etc. the more quickly they are either going to be attracted to want to do business with you, or realize that you are not the best fit for them. You're both going to find this out eventually, so why not know sooner rather than later? Take a risk. I understand the fear is that you will scare people off too early and actually have less new business opportunities. My experience tells me that the opposite actually happens.

Aren't you tired of trying to break through the clutter of the marketplace, sounding like everyone else, when in your heart and mind you know you are different and do provide unique value? Risk being more bold and clear about who is and is not a good fit to do business with you and your organization. This kind of approach in and of itself will differentiate you from the competition, because your competitors are all struggling with these same things.

Key Reminders:

- Risk scaring prospects off with more specific, meaningful information about why people hire you – 'spin them in' or 'spin them out' and learn to be ok with either one.

- Be clear and bold about who you are, what you do and how you see things (without "selling") – break through the clutter of the marketplace and sounding like everyone else.

- Your language, tone and overall approach with new prospects will differentiate you from the competition as much as your specific product or service.

YOU ATTRACT WHAT YOU DEFINE

Preview Points:

- Dating analogy: Find the right partner quicker. Waste less time on dates that you know, in the end, are not going to work out.
- Stay focused and specific about what you are looking to attract "more of" over time and you are guaranteed to get it.
- Minimize the buzzwords and corporate speak. Be specific, compelling, and human when you discuss the kind of new business you are looking for "more of."

More than just getting new business, the primary obstacle and resulting opportunity I have found in my business consulting career is around generating the right kinds of new business. The profitable, growth-oriented, interesting projects and accounts that can help fuel my organization's growth.

Ideal *(adjective)*: conceived as constituting a standard of perfection or excellence: *ideal beauty.* regarded as perfect of its kind: *an ideal spot for a home.*

Are you focusing on building a pipeline of more *ideal* clients? Do you know who your *ideal* clients are? Do you know how much of your current business comes from your *ideal* clients? Do you know what percent of time and energy you spend supporting these clients compared to others? Being clear about what *bad* business looks like is equally important to knowing what *ideal* business looks like. Sometimes knowing when to walk away is as important, and financially impactful, as closing the deal. In this age when customers have more power, it's easy to get thrown off balance and give them control over the process, the price, etc.

There are hundreds of sales books and training programs that talk about defining your ideal client and being more bold around spending more time calling higher, leveraging your best clients, etc. I have never come across any business professional or organization that said they were doing business with enough ideal clients and didn't need any more.

Do you know where your growth is currently coming from, or where it will come from? What current clients of yours are most apt to fuel your growth — with new business and quality referrals? Which of your current clients would you like to duplicate; to find "more of these kinds of people" to work with? At the risk of stating the obvious, your revenue, profit, and income growth is not going to come from your less profitable, more difficult, "C" clients. As you are prospecting for new business, make certain you are clear about exactly what you are, and are not, looking for. Can you talk off the top of your head with clarity and an ability to *paint a picture* of what you seek that anyone (your prospects, referral sources/network, clients) can easily understand?

Getting clear about what an *ideal* or "A" client looks like in your business (juxtaposed with a *less than ideal* or "C" client) is a simple task that I find most in business make difficult. Take some time to specifically define what kinds of people and companies you'd like to do business with. I'm sure you have done this before, but I would ask that you take it one layer deeper. The more you are reading, thinking, and talking about these things, the better chance you will have of creating the right kinds of opportunities that match your list.

Here are a few samples of actual "A" client lists. Some of the descriptors are tangible and business-focused; others are more intangible and personalized. There is no right or wrong way to do this, use the method that best suits your needs. I find most professionals responsible for developing new business are not specific or personal enough in their descriptors of the kinds of "A" clients they would like to attract "more of." Even successful professionals often have trouble believing they have a right to be specific and set stringent standards for what they are looking for. They are just "happy to have the opportunity to compete" for each piece of business. It has been my experience that this kind of "one-down" position runs rampant in the business world.

I offer the below real-time lists to challenge you to create an updated one of your own. I want these lists to stimulate your growth over the course of the next year. What kinds of people and organizations are you looking for "more of?" Be specific. The marketplace is abundant. There are plenty more of these out there that you are currently not doing business with. What's holding you back?

I Am Looking to Attract "More Of..."

I find it essential to personalize this list, make it pop, come alive. You should be able to see this person, to feel and know what it's like to work with them. I assume you have a couple of "A" clients you can model your list after. You can also create a composite description based on the traits of some of your best clients.

"A" CLIENT Example 1: Wholesale Floral & Floral Supply (Sales / Client Service Rep)

I am attracting "MORE OF"...

- 5 new customers who purchase $10K+ per month and 10 new customers who purchase $4K+ per month within the next 12 months, or less.
- Customers willing to engage, allow us into their business.
- Truly open and interested in doing new things.
- Are hungry for a partner and different programs.
- Bouquet makers and large scale wholesalers who service over 350 customers.

The person who created this list above at the beginning of our work together sent me an unsolicited note a year later on his progress.

"I was walking through the sales floor this morning and realized I had no time to deal with 2-3 box orders anymore (physically, not enough time in my day for it). I have way too many big customers who need me to give them attention. My next thought was… remember when you defined what you wanted? Well, it took a year or so, but I've got what I want (not all, but well on my way). This really works. Last year this time I sold $125,000 for the month of March. This year, with less time and more responsibilities, I will sell roughly $235,000."

— Kevin Romani, Business Development Manager

"A" CLIENT Example 2: Market Research Company
(President & Business Development Team)

"We are looking to attract more companies that..."

Tangibles

- Conduct market research or have a need / want to conduct market research
- Decision Maker – person currently in charge of market research
- Have immediate need (within next 3 months)
- Have marketing budget of $500,000+ per year
- Projecting growth of 20% minimum in next fiscal year
- End Users, Research Companies, PR / Ad agencies
- Established (3+ years in business)

Intangibles

- Interested in long term partnership
- Wants vendor involved in research process
- Willing to give us the time to get to know their pain and challenges
- Have not yet found effective, reliable research source for market research
- Not looking for just the best price
- Open to feedback and ideas on most effective way to conduct research
- Looking for sole / single research vendor
- Pays bills on time
- Sees value in us

"A" CLIENT Example 3: Professional Services Firm (Partner Group)

New clients that are the best fit for us are...
- Big enough so they can afford us ($5-50 million business or high net worth individuals)
- Strong industry background overall, weak in business finance
- Profitable, growing, good capital base
- Active management group involved in the business (no absentee owner)
- Ethical
- Progressive in thinking
- Willing to work with us as a team
- Want to grow, care about the future
- Open to take risks (or at least not too risk averse)
- Business owner passionate about success of product and company. View their work as important (not just a job).
- Financially healthy, solvent, good cash flow
- Use multiple services of ours and open to other work/support
- Return calls promptly and forthcoming with all the information we need and ask for
- Willing to listen to our advice and apply it
- Do not complain about money / invoices and pay in timely manner
- Fun to work with, always optimistic

"A" CLIENT Example 4: Financial Services Professional

New clients that are the best fit for us are...

- Married with children — healthy, stable relationships
- No debt or manageable debt
- $500,000+ in assets
- Clear idea about their future
- Truly open to change and new ideas
- Listens to me, trusts my advice
- Driven, goal-oriented
- Disciplined, able to stick to a plan (no knee-jerk reactions)
- Aspirations for a better future (optimistic)
- Well-networked - will naturally refer friends, family, and colleagues

---

The next example is a different spin on the original idea. As you are defining and clarifying the kinds of people and companies you want to attract "more of," it's important to get comfortable with the idea that you have expectations of your clients. The earlier you orient them to this, the easier it will be to work with them moving forward. Your business relationship is not a one-way street. Just because they pay you for your services doesn't mean they have all the control and call all the shots. You have solutions and resources that are valuable to them. Your time and energy is valuable.

Notice any places where you are falling into the trap of working with "C" clients that drain your time and energy and are not very profitable. I'm not suggesting that you can't have "C" clients; I am suggesting that your business growth will NOT come from "C" clients. Growth will come from "A's" and maybe some "B's" that have "A" potential. If you want to grow, take a good hard look at who your clients are and what kinds of clients you need to attract "more of" to meet your growth goals. Also consider the idea that you can "expect" things from your clients, just as they "expect" things from you. Is any of this out of balance in your business?

Example 5: Technology Company
(President)

Expectations We Have of Our Clients:

· They must accept/realize that we know more than they do (in our specialized areas) and that we will use our knowledge to develop products to support their best interests. It's better if a client doesn't act like they know the perfect solution that we should implement or direct the tools that we would use to support them. They must trust us and our intent.

· Clients that have money to spend (not a continual battle for payment or constant negotiation on rates / level of effort). They are not short sighted about money. We believe we are a best value firm in that we provide exceptional service for a fair cost (but we are not the cheapest).

· They either need to have clearly defined requirements or give us a smaller task to define them.

· Be fun to interact with - not too stuffy yet know when to be serious about business.

· Clients that have continual technology improvement programs - not afraid to adopt technology but are not stupid about spending money for the sake of spending.

They see technology as their weapon and need to spend money wisely to maximize our effectiveness without introducing too much risk.

· Clients that either enjoy their market position or aspire to improve this position and understand that money needs to be spent in order to maintain and increase their market position.

Remember both your time and theirs is valuable. Help your clients more quickly put you in a category of "Yes, I am interested in learning more and think we might be a good fit," or "You know what, I don't think we are a fit." Sometimes this will seem counter-intuitive. Attract people into your process and spin out people who aren't good fits. You have nothing to hide and are not in the business of trying to force people into things they are not open to or interested in. The clearer you are up front about who you are looking for and what you are and are not, the less time you and your prospect will waste on "the dance." Although simple in theory, I find most professionals who are responsible for developing business don't do an effective job of this up front.

I prefer to stay positive and focus on what you are looking to attract, what you expect, what you want "more of," and who you are. Occasionally, to make this point, you can also juxtapose this with a few brief, bold statements about what you are NOT. Being seemingly self critical does take confidence in your unique market position. This approach is another way to get focused on your core strengths and strategic differentiators. If there are "perceived weaknesses," I find it's best to get them out on the table right up front. If you speak to these perceptions before your client does, you retain some level of control and high ground. If your prospect starts picking at you, putting you on the spot, and telling you what you don't have, it is easy to get subservient and defensive.

If telling them what you are not scares them off, so be it. Eventually, they were going to be scared off anyway. It is better for this to happen earlier in the process, so everyone involved wastes less time.

Here is one example of some of the "what we are NOT" phrases that a professional services firm weaves into their initial conversations with new prospects when appropriate:

What We Are Not Examples

- The flashiest people with the slickest PowerPoint presentations and Fortune 500 clients.
- The cheapest.
- We do not have the highest profile national name recognition.
- We are not a good fit for startup companies.
- If our first project is something you want turned around last minute we probably won't be able to help you.

If there is one thing that most all of my clients have in common, it's that they are not the lowest price provider. They are competitive in their respective markets, but at times can be more expensive than much of their competition. If you are going to be more expensive, relative to what your client is used to, tell them right up front. Let them know what to expect. At least plant the seed to remind them that they are going to get lower prices from others. As long as your product / service has unique value and you are taking them through a process that helps you differentiate yourself and helps them understand why it would make sense to pay more to work with you, this will play to your favor. If you are the lowest price provider and this is your primary selling point, you are not reading this book. I find most people and companies who can benefit from these approaches to sales, business communication, and personal achievement are providing a high quality product or service and are charging a premium for it. They have unique value, provide high levels of client service, care about what they do, and the clients they work for.

How You Are Spending Your Time & What is Your Return with Existing Clients?

"The law of flotation was not discovered by contemplating the sinking of things, but by contemplating the floating of things, which floated naturally, and then intelligently asking why they did so."
— Thomas Troward, as quoted in The Power of Intention by Wayne Dyer

Putting your clients in buckets: A - B - C. Another useful exercise is to take a hard look at your clients and identify the qualities of the A's (ideal clients you want more of), B's (good clients that have the potential to be A's), and C's (lower margin, resource heavy clients you are not looking for more of). We will focus on the A's and C's. Taking a hard look at and "bucketing" your current clients will help you and improve your process for talking about and qualifying new prospects. It will help you identify the red flags to watch for that indicate a "C" client. I am assuming that in your new business efforts, you are not actively looking for more "C" clients but rather in attracting more "A" and "B" business. This is where the revenue and profitability and right projects for growth live.

Client Buckets Example 1: Defining the A-B-C Buckets

"A" Clients are:

- Consistent throughout the year.
- Open to conversation (business or personal).
- Proactive in wanting info, pricing, programs.
- Challenging (in a good way) to me.
- A "partnership" relationship.
- Respectful.
- Quality is more important than price to them.

"B" Clients are:

- Around during the holidays.
- Open to limited conversation (business only).
- More "last second" in their preparations and needs.
- A "commodity" relationship.
- Less progressive.
- Price driven.

"C" Clients are:

- Very unorganized.
- Hard to get a hold of.
- Standoffish.
- Not open to change.
- No "Real" relationship.
- Price driven.

Client Buckets Example 2: Describing the Buckets

"A" client descriptions

- Partner.
- Firm believer (advocate).
- Value us, use us on a regular basis.
- Can make decisions – they have control of the $$$.
- Turn to us – we are top of mind.
  Respect us and our perspective.
- Work together well – profitable for both parties.
- There is potential for growth.
- Brutal honesty.
- Low maintenance.
- Integrate us into their business.
- Demanding yet fair.

Sometimes I will skip the B's. It's most important to define those on each end of the spectrum, the clients you want more of and fewer of.

"C" client descriptions

- See themselves as superior. Unwilling to take advice/ follow a process.
- Don't recognize value.
- Don't respect what you do – no boundaries.
- Don't know what they want.
- Not communicating.
- Resource suck.
- Everything is "Wait" or "Can't wait!"
- Urgency is everything – seems like "life or death."

I had a client tell me they analyzed all five hundred of their clients. **They found that their top fifty clients provide 87% of their total business.** This group also has a higher average growth rate, 18%, than any others. This is where the growth is going to come: Developing more business from this top 10%, AND focusing new business development efforts on finding MORE of these *ideal* clients.

In the work that I do with professional organizations, uncovering nuggets like these can have a profound effect on how they organize their business and allot time and energy. My job is to challenge you to look at your business with fresh eyes and to face the harsh realities of where your growth is really going to come from and where you are currently wasting time. In my experience, the best clients that make up significant portions of a company's revenue often take significantly less time and energy proportionate to their return. You can make more money with less effort.

Not too long ago, one of my clients sent me a note about a review he had with one of his sales reps. As they dug into this particular rep's clients, they discovered that **his top two customers do 50% of his business and take up about 5% of his time.** This realization helped him re-think and focus the majority of his efforts toward developing more business within these clients as well as looking at finding prospective new clients that fit a similar profile.

Related to your "C" prospects, weeding them out means more quickly identifying the "red flags." When you are dating, you are scanning for and noting red flags. Certain behaviors (i.e.: how they dress, how they talk, what they ask, how they interact with others, personal mannerisms, etc.) are leading indicators about whether this person is a match with you or not. It's not that you can't look past them or want to judge them too harshly or too quickly. You do, however, get constant clues about who this person is and whether or not you think they are a good fit for you. After a short period of time you have a really good idea if this first date will lead to second one or not. Occasionally, it turns out, you misread the cues and judge them incorrectly (or maybe they did this to you). It might take more than one date to get enough information, of course, but, the first date sets the foundation for everything that will or will not follow. It's the same when working with a new business prospect.

As you develop a healthy sense of skepticism and are not just "happy to have the opportunity" to get some new business, create your "red flags" list. What are the things you want to watch for? What are the leading indicators that you have found most often lead to someone not being a good fit? It doesn't mean you won't talk with them or consider engaging with them. It does mean that you are going to be very careful about how much time and energy you put into your preparation and interaction with them, and how flexible you are with your engagement process in relation to their process for selection. I would like you to be a little tougher on what you deem to be possible "C" prospects. You can be respectful and nice, of course. But, I'd like you to ask even tougher questions and also be willing to walk away. Remember, being willing to walk away from bad business is as important as finding good business. The two are inextricably linked.

Example of a possible "C" Prospective Client **Red Flags**

- "Request for Proposal" with no opportunity to ask questions or meet.
- Very quick timeline for your turnaround of RFP, yet unclear timeline for their response.
- Demanding, very impersonal.

- Cost is primary focus.
- RFP that goes out to more than three other organizations.

You Get What You Tolerate

I find that the reason most people tolerate lots of less-than-ideal clients and spend so much of time working on bad opportunities is that they don't understand their value. Look at your clients. How many of them do you enjoy working with? How many of them value your product / service, pay you on time, and are good to work with? This doesn't mean they don't challenge and push you, of course, but that they are professional, respectful, and willing to pay for your unique value.

Question: What are you tolerating?

What drives your willingness to put up with things that you probably shouldn't? I know when I get caught here, it's usually because I get attached to money and am afraid to let go. This is a trap. The more you hold on tightly to the wrong people, the wrong clients, and the wrong prospective deals, the more you hold yourself back. You get caught in a pattern of mediocrity and send a message that you are willing to tolerate getting beat down on price, treated poorly, and not paid on time. Perhaps you don't have any of these kinds of client relationships or prospects like this in the hopper. If that's the case, good for you. Consider how this might be relevant for anyone else on your team.

"People who are already successful became so precisely because they were unwilling to tolerate certain aspects of their job they didn't like. Their intolerance caused their success... The point here is simply that you will contribute the most, as either an individual performer or a team member, when your role closely matches your strengths, and that it's your responsibility to try to arrange your world so that it does... The most successful people sculpt their jobs so that they spend a disproportionate amount of time doing what they love... the moment you are spending less than 70% of your time on the things you love to do, identify the activities getting in the way and take action to remove them."

—Marcus Buckingham, The One Thing You Need to Know

Below is a note from a client that got stuck in a subservient position with walk-in clients that were not respecting her process or their client – advisor professional agreements. She realized that was putting her in a position that, in the end, didn't serve her, or her clients.

"I am here to serve my clients, and at the same time I need to have agreements, expectations, and processes in place to work effectively and keep myself sane, too. I used to tolerate clients walking in or calling and expecting service for whatever their needs were at that moment. The problem was that I was often with another client at the time or in the middle of a client-related project. I had the habit of being overly accommodating to them, to the point that it became a disruption to my day, agenda, priorities, etc. I decided to make a change and retrain my clients. Now, when they walk-in/call-in, my assistant instructs them that they need to schedule an appointment if they want to meet with me. Of course, unless it is truly something life-threateningly urgent. If my assistant determines they do not need an appointment and she can assist them, then she does so. This new process has freed me up to better focus on my immediate priorities and to be more present with and helpful to my clients."

One of the things I find when I'm in the new client nego-tiation process is that people tend to want to go right to the information for information's sake — *what is the price, who else do you work with, why should we work with you, what are your credentials?* Does any of this information really help prospects understand if we have a good fit and if we can solve their problems? Do they really even know why they're asking? Aren't there some things that would be more useful to ask about, talk about, and listen for? Now, I'm not suggesting that we go back to the days of the three martini lunch and golf outings every other day. I am suggesting that there are ways to be effective and efficient with our time, while also not leaving out the human element of sales, negotiation, and business communication.

As humans, we are emotional creatures first and foremost. We have personal and emotional reasons for taking all actions, especially new ones. There are very compelling reasons we have for considering change and genuine costs (tangible and intan-gible) to not changing. We have fears, concerns, and excite-ment about new opportunities. We may be open to asking for and getting help, and at the same time we have some fear of making a mistake or getting taken advantage of. We want to make sure we get a good deal and don't want to pay "too much" for something. This can lead to significant short-sightedness on the part of the buyer. At the same time, as the seller, you have to be more psychologically savvy about what's going on for your prospects and find ways to get them to open up and tell you the truth. Being direct and genuine with a clear process will help us toward that goal.

Many business professionals spend much of their time working on the flashy PowerPoint deck and learning all the details of the prospect's business in preparation for the "big presentation." Some of this is necessary to look and sound professional, of course, but often it gets taken way too far.

Sometimes what's most important is uncovering something as simple as why your new prospect is considering a change; what they have to gain or lose by doing something different. For all the time we spend feeding clients with information about how many gigabytes per minute our machines can process, how many advanced degrees our consultants have, and bragging about our *A-list* clients, maybe we should spend a few minutes on some simple, key questions that would help clarify if there is any kind of fit.

We will talk more in future chapters about language, key questions and having your own process for engaging new clients. This first list is designed to plant the seed in your head that it is OK to be more skeptical and strategic about your approach for engaging with new prospects. Here are some things you can say and ask to ensure right up front that you are not wasting each other's time. Some of these questions and comments are things you might actually ask or say to a prospective new client. Others are more of an ideal checklist to keep in mind, as well as things to be discussed with your team internally. Create your own version of this list when considering new business opportunities. Use your time and energy wisely. There is only so much of it to go around.

Key Questions to Establish a Good Fit

- Can we identify some problems or opportunities that you have, and can I share something about what we do that is relevant and connected to what you might need?
- Do I trust you, like you, see that I'd like to do business with you? (Subsequently, do you, Mr. Prospect, trust Me? Do I seem competent?)
- Do you have a truly compelling reason to change and is the cost to not changing greater than the cost to taking the risk of doing something different?
- How do you fit into my Ideal Client profile?

- Do I have a process for engaging new prospects and if so, what elements of my process are flexible and what elements are not?

- Do you have a process for engaging new vendor / partners and is it flexible?

- Do you have the power to make a decision, or are there others that need to be involved and that have a stake in seeing this problem get solved or this opportunity brought to fruition?

- Am I willing to walk away from potential business if you are unwilling to follow certain parts of my process? Do I have the courage to do this?

- Are there any difficult conversations you, Mr. Prospect, are going to have to have with bosses, board members, and/or existing vendor / partners around making a change?

- What is it about our conversations that leads you to think we might have a good fit?

- What's still missing and concerns you? me? What else do I need to hear / see in order to feel comfortable about doing business together?

- What's your lifetime value as a client to me? What's my lifetime value as a solution provider to you?

- Is there anyone else (existing vendor/partner, peer or boss or board member) that might make a last minute push to keep things the way they are or try to save the account and the status quo? Are you prepared for that?

- Where else am I getting pressure to close the deal? If this is happening (in my own head or from a boss, board, spouse) am I aware of how that might be affecting my ability to execute my process?

Most professionals responsible for developing new business spend far too little time working on solidifying their process and approach for engaging new prospects. Most are not aware of their own mindset and emotions going into an important meeting. Many have not mastered the art of asking really good questions, ensuring they are in control, and talking to all the right people. In order to generate that next level of results and success it is essential that you understand why your best clients buy from you and what situations they were in when they first decided to do business with you. It's a simple formula.

In order to grow your business, a certain amount of activity is of course important. The right kind of activity is more important. Work to develop your sense of focus and ability to communicate who your *ideal* clients are. The more precise your ability to identify and focus your plan for attracting more *ideal* clients, the more of a chance you will actually get them.

Key Reminders:

• In order to grow your business, a certain amount of activity is of course important. The RIGHT kind of activity is exponentially more important to achieve high levels of growth and maintain your sanity.

• Focus your energy and effort on thinking, writing and talking about who your ideal clients are. Notice resistance and do it anyway.

• Work on any 'emotional baggage' you might have around your worth and addiction to things needing to be hard. Use these exercises as an opportunity to acknowledge and begin making important changes in your thinking.

EFFECTIVE LANGUAGE FOR GETTING RESPONSES & GETTING THE TRUTH

Preview Points:

- You talk too much, no matter what you might think.
- You cannot force or manipulate anyone to do anything they don't want to do.
- Find the motive for change and everything else is easy.
- Relax, lose the mask you think you need. Be genuine.

Get a Response and Get the Truth

My experience is that most business professionals are generally lazy with their written and spoken language. These busy, demanding times require a new level of awareness and sophistication in your business communication, especially in new business-related efforts. I'm going to make this section very practical, focusing on specific words, phrases, as well as email and phone language structure to guide your efforts to engage new prospects.

Business professionals are writing (emails, instant messages, text messages) more than ever before. We are also leaving more voice mail messages since it's next to impossible to catch people in their office and have them pick up the phone without an appointment. It is harder than ever to get a prospect's attention.

~~Email & V~~ice Mail Observations

~~Before we w~~ork through my detailed language suggestions, let me first frame out my general observations about conventional new business prospecting communication through email, voice mail, and phone conversations.

1. Emails and voice mails are too long. They give too much information. Business and sales professionals often fear if they don't *data dump* right away, they may never get another chance. They fill their messages with LOTS of general information that the prospect either cannot process or just tunes out.

2. At the end of the email or voice mail there is no clear offer and proposed next step. If you are going to get people to respond or commit to something, they need to know exactly what they are committing to. If you are asking them to agree to something, keeping the scope of their commitment short with minimal expectations will improve your chances of getting a yes.

3. Most business and sales professionals are afraid of language that appears negative or weak. Phrases such as "I don't know," "You don't know me," "I have no idea," and "I'm not sure" can cause initial panic for those responsible for getting people to say yes. Without some version of these phrases, there is no "space" for the prospect to relax and actually listen to what you have to say.

4. Most humans have a hard time knowing when and how to "walk away." Sometimes you have done all you can. If you are not getting a response, even if they showed interest at one time, you have to learn when and how to walk away.

5. People are afraid to make anyone uncomfortable or mad. This leads to what I call an "over-politeness" in email and voice mail and puts you in a "one-down," subservient position. It can also lead to passive-aggressive communication with emotional undercurrents that are very ineffective at getting a truthful response.

6. When in "sales mode," most professionals feel compelled to use excited language with an overly positive tone. They feel as if they need to get people excited about their product or service and display high levels of confidence in their value. This approach often backfires quickly.

7. When in "sales mode," most professionals get caught using leading statements intended to cajole the prospect into action. The prospect is never given an out.

8. Use of meaningless business speak, buzzwords, and other language that is missing a more human, conversational tone.

9. There is no upfront clarification of intent and expectations. When a prospect knows what to expect, they are more likely to stay open to listen to and participate in what comes next.

10. Most professionals responsible for developing new business forget that the goal and intent of an initial prospecting email or voice mail is to:
    • Get a response.
    • Get the truth.
    • Move forward to the next step -or-
      Move on, go your separate ways.

The most profound change I will ask you to consider making in your sales-related communication is to STOP doing and saying the things that put you in a "one-down" position (i.e.: a position of weakness, "not good enough," just happy to get the opportunity to win the business). Growing up, we all learned to be nice and polite, always saying "please" and "thank you." Somewhere we also learned that in business you have to sound excited and kiss everyone's butt. I do not agree. I believe there are things we do and say that actually hurt our chances of getting more of the right kinds of new business. I am all for being professional and cordial, but I believe we must be more disciplined about our language and subtle messages it sends — especially since it's harder and harder to actually speak directly to someone these days. I am interested in how we can better communicate from a position of equality with prospects and clients.

Review your email, voice mail, phone, and face-to-face communication for these words and phrases. They will not help you win more new business or negotiate from a position of equality.

Let's get to some examples. All of these phrases and emails below were written by real people. Some are from clients of mine at the beginning of an engagement. Others are examples my clients have found and sent to me because they know I get a twisted enjoyment out of collecting BAD sales emails. Seeing some of these might make you mad. You may currently be using some of these words and phrases in your prospect and client communication. All I ask is that you keep an open mind and consider the impact that these subtle shifts in language might have on your results.

- "Thanks for your time."
- "I would like to see if I could setup a 30 minute call with you in the near future..."

- "Please let me know if this sounds acceptable."
- "I look forward to hearing from you!" (when you have no prior agreement or relationship)
- "The reason for my note is to request a brief 30 minute call with you to see how *&*# can best support your online business needs in 2006."
- "I will call you tomorrow to show you how we can help you win more business."
- "… would greatly appreciate being considered for your upcoming research projects."
- "Thank you for taking a few minutes to speak with me today."
- "Thank you for taking a look at what we have to offer."
- "!" (Exclamation points)
- "Please."
- "I look forward to working with you." *(note: This was sent after one exploratory call and NO commitment or agreement)*
- "I wanted to let you know that we are now in a position to give you a proposal and would love to have the opportunity to do so."
- "We look forward to working with you on this!"
- "Thank you for this exciting opportunity!" *(note: This was sent after one exploratory call and no commitment or agreement.)*
- "Thank you for the opportunity to serve you."
- "I would like the opportunity to provide you with a quote for any upcoming projects you may have."
- "If we are not currently working together, maybe we should be!"
- "Hopefully."
- "I would love to have the chance to work with you."

Bad Email Examples
Why they are bad, and things to watch for.

As you are reading these, watch for the words and phrases that put the person one-down. Use the above checklist as a reference.

Remember, these are all real emails from well-intended, high functioning business professionals and salespeople that got no response. Maybe you have never said these things or maybe you say them all the time. Either way, the more aware you can be of the subtleties of your language, the better.

Following this section, we will talk about alternative phrases and how to make these emails more effective. But first, let's focus on what doesn't work.

(Any use of company or individual's names below, have been changed so as not to embarrass them.)

Bad Email Example 1

Good Morning,

I attempted to call and speak to you personally regarding this matter.

I'd like to speak with you and set up an appointment and or demonstration with you about how our Communications Solutions can lower your total cost of ownership.

X Networks can help your company lower your total cost of ownership by combining voice and Internet service with one provider.

That's one bill for voice, broadband, conferencing, email, and Web hosting.

Voice Services include local and long distance services and free inter-office calling. X Networks can work with or replace your existing PBX or Key system.

We can reduce your total communication costs for voice and broadband while simplifying administration and management.

Please feel free to call at the number below, should you have any further questions. I really look forward to your response. Thank you, and make it a great day!

Feedback on Bad Email Example 1

- No clear next step.
- All push, telling them what they can do, with no qualifying information.
- Assuming a response ("I really look forward to").

- "Thank you" — for what?
- "Make it a great day" is fine for people that you know. Sounds a bit cheesy and trying too hard to be extra positive to people that don't know you.

Bad Email Example 2

Hi Chris,

My name is Adam Brady and I am on the business development team at Pointe Solutions Research.

The reason for my note is to request a brief 20 minute call with you to see how we can better support your research needs moving forward in 2006. We've recently invested in enhancing our profiling, validation, and security, in addition to several other exciting improvements which I'd like to share with you.

Please let me know your availability to talk in the next week. I look forward to the opportunity to learn more about your research needs and share with you in more detail about our capabilities. My contact information is below, and I look forward to hearing from you at your earliest convenience.

Feedback on Bad Email Example 2

- Assumptive - no opportunity for prospect to be "open to" anything. All push. No reference to what the salesperson "doesn't know."
- No clear next step.
- "Please" is a word that people use and they are not even aware of it. In these instances, it is totally unnecessary. It is a subtle begging word.

Bad Email Example 3

Dear Linda,

Thank you for taking a few minutes to speak with me today. I've attached the information I promised and I will follow up with you later this week. I can appreciate your loyalty to your current vendors and thank you for taking a look at what we have to offer.

My background before working here at J&C was with a wholesaler for almost 10 years. I am very loyal to the wholesale community and do whatever I can to partner with my customers in order to maximize sales.

Have a great afternoon!

Feedback on Bad Email Example 3

- Stop thanking people for their time. Is their time more valuable than yours, really?
- Stop thanking people for looking at your stuff or considering your organization.
- No reference to any kind of near or longer term next step.
- Exclamation points (!), unnecessary and often not genuine, especially if you don't know the person.

Bad Email Example 4

Hi Kent,

I thought I would touch base with you about the progress of a couple of things here at STR Solutions. We will be bringing the XTX Worldwide system in-house this year. It's expected to be a six month project, so we'll be looking at third quarter.

When we spoke in December you mentioned you'd be interested in a proposal for PIN-based debit processing. I wanted to let you know that we are now in a position to give you a proposal and would love to have the opportunity to do so. It hasn't been announced yet, but we are expanding our relationship with Bank American to support this additional set of transactions. I believe you said that your current contract is up for renewal in late 2006. I know most of the EFT processors require six months notice, so I suspect time is of the essence for you.

With our one-stop debit offering we can process your current networks. We are putting an emphasis on sharing with our clients the advantage of a complete brand debit strategy though. There are extremely compelling financial advantages and our proposal to you will include them. The financial advantages we can share with you will far outweigh their fee.

Stacey in my office will follow-up with you on the debit presentation and proposal. In the meantime, please don't hesitate to contact me directly if you have questions about this or other matters. We look forward to working with you on this!

Feedback on Bad Email Example 4

- Way too long.
- Uses the word "love" (i.e.: "would love to have the opportunity") which automatically puts him one-down.
- Assumptive (i.e.: "we look forward to working with you on this!") when there is no agreement in place or current dialogue.
- Exclamation points ("!")
- No clear next step.

Bad Email Example 5

Roy,

Thank you for requesting the White Paper on our Training Solutions Products. While this is an automated response from the website - I've set it up to send from my personal email. Your interest in our new program is very important to me so I've been cc'd to this note and I would love to personally follow up with you.

If you've had a chance to view the video clips, you will agree with me that this is unlike anything that the training industry has delivered before. I have personally been involved with the interventions with Yahoo!, Coca-Cola, Hilton, and Best Buy. I welcome the opportunity to connect with you for a brief conference call to tell you more about how our training program experience can work for your organization.

Please review the attached PDF White Paper and I will be in touch with you shortly. If time is of essence to you - I've enclosed both my business phone and cell for faster service.

Thank you for the opportunity to serve you.

Feedback on Bad Email Example 5

- "I would love to personally follow up with you."
  Remove emotional words like "love" and anything
  that seems over-eager.
- "I welcome the opportunity to connect with you…"
  Assumptive, and not a clear next step.
- "I will be in touch with you shortly."
  Not a clear next step. Process is confusing.
- "Thank you for the opportunity to serve you."
  Assumptive at this stage, and places her in
  "One-Down" position.

I believe in selling 180 degrees differently than most have been taught. I actually believe you can sell more by not selling, not pushing, and not assuming. These emails all push and assume. Everyone in sales talks and writes too much. It is imperative that you give less info than you feel compelled to give up front. You just need to give enough to get the meeting. Offer clear and concise statements about what you do and who you do it for. Tell your prospects who you are right up front. You are trying to get them to stay open to read your email and not tune out this "salesperson" standing in front of them. As quickly as possible talk about something that might draw their attention and is relevant to their world. Don't talk about how great your company is *in a vacuum*. Relate it to something that references your prospect's situation. What most sales people miss is that they have no idea if this prospect is open to talk with them, or if any of this information is relevant or of interest to them. I believe it's important to state that, or some version of it, each time.

Eliminate one-down phrases like "I would like the opportunity" and "Thank you." Get rid of assumptive phrases like "I know there are opportunities." You don't know that, because you haven't heard from them yet. You don't know what they care about. You "think" there "may" be some opportunities. I understand you may feel strongly about the potential relationship and the reasons why it makes sense. You may feel that you have to be bold and confident right up front to get their attention. I don't think this works anymore. You have to temper that certainty and excitement, or your prospect is apt to immediately resist you because they sense a "salesperson" or a "know-it-all."

Here is an effective example that takes these things into consideration. This can be used as an email, a voice mail, or during phone communication. Ideally, if you cannot speak to your client live, you can use this as a voice mail and email it immediately afterwards to increase your chances of getting a response. (*Individual and company names below have been changed to protect confidentiality.*)

Effective Email Example

Hi Nina,

My name is Jack Bowen. I am the Vice President of Client Services with T&C Floral Supplies in Philadelphia. You have no idea who I am.

We currently have a relationship with twenty Giant Foods stores in the Northeast providing regionally customized and seasonal floral supplies. In talking to some of your floral managers it seems there may be opportunities for sourcing new, unique products, developing programs, and saving you money.

I don't have any idea if you're looking at new products and new ideas these days or if you're happy with what you're doing and reaching your goals for the year.

I am writing to see if you might be open to schedule a brief, 15-minute conversation. My intent would be to find out if any of what we do might be relevant and helpful to reaching your new product initiatives and financial goals for '07. I will be in town next week if we want to meet briefly face-to-face, or we can also talk via phone if you prefer. Let me know either way if this is something you're open to (or not).

Sincerely, Jack

By asking if the person is "open" and using words that give them some responsibility in deciding like "might," you set yourself up to have more of a mutually motivated dialogue. This way might at first seem weak or give your prospect an out. I can tell you from personal experience that it is the best way to ensure you get the meeting and that they are "bought in" and not cajoled or forced. The more buy-in your prospect has, the more of a chance you have of them opening up to you and sharing all the information you need. We cannot assume they are open to talk, ever.

Here is a quick summary of the "Don'ts" and other guiding principles for email and voice mail language. Which ones do you think you are most guilty of using? (*Check all that apply.*)

Email and Voice Mail Don'ts

___ Thank You + Thank you for your time

___ Please

___ Emotional words i.e.: "love," "excited" or exclamation points ("!")

___ Statements that put you "one-down" (i.e.: "We would greatly appreciate being considered," or, "Thank you for the opportunity to serve you.")

___ Way too much info, too long

___ Info about your company that is not meaningful (i.e.: "We are a clear leader.")

___ Assuming that they are going to call you back (i.e.: Not giving them an out and using phrases like "if you are open to it...")

___ No clear next step

___ Anything that is not genuine, is salesy, that you would never say normally in your personal life.

Watch your words in all your written and spoken communication. Be more aware of and disciplined about them in all client interactions.

Now, let's get into it in a little more detail. Here are some examples of a "Before" and "After." I want to stress that there is no perfect email. Each one is different depending on the situation. I am pointing out some themes that I see in the structure of, intent behind, and language within emails and phone and voice mail scripts that I have seen from countless professionals who are responsible for developing new business.

Language That Creates Space to Get the Truth

In a moment, we'll look at some words and phrases that create space. By "creating space" I mean they minimize the automatic resistance or eliminate the wall that comes up immediately if someone doesn't know you and isn't sure what you want from them. The wall is especially quick and tough to penetrate if people think you are contacting them to "sell" them something. In sales we are often taught to use forceful, confident, and assumptive language. I am suggesting a different approach that will give you a better chance of the prospect staying open to hear your request and give you a truthful answer, as well as give you the best chance to get a meeting or next step. Creating space is designed to have them meet you half way, as opposed to you pushing for what you want. If we can get people to meet us half way we are much more likely to close business and waste less time with prospects that are not open minded.

I don't know about you, but I get tired of spinning my wheels. I want to deal with people that are open to talk, interested in new ideas, and have some kind of need in the areas that I can help them. The words and phrases listed below disarm people, allow them to let their defenses down, and then consider following our lead to the next step (if we both agree it makes sense to move forward). The idea is that we want to stay out of the "salesperson box" that most people get stuck in. Once you get put in that box (i.e.: you are there to push something on them they don't want or don't have time to talk about), the defenses go up and people shut down. The right or wrong word here or there can help you keep them open to considering what you have to offer, or close them off to hearing you at all (even if you might have a genuine solution to their need). Notice any judgment you (or your ego) might have to some of these words being "passive" and remember that the intent is to close more business, not less. You will have to trust me that the proper use of these words, along with the right intent, mindset, and strong client engagement process, will lead to you getting more new business from new prospects and existing clients.

For those of you that don't consider yourselves salespeople, you might find that you don't make certain calls or send emails to prospects, potential strategic partners, or referrals because you don't want to come across like a salesperson. There is no magic pill to make you comfortable reaching out to people that don't know you. Despite my experience, I still don't feel 100% comfortable doing that. I have found that some of these key words and phrases can make it feel a little more real, honest, direct, and non-salesy. This, ideally, makes you a little more willing to engage in activity that can help you grow your business from new prospects and existing clients.

One last note. These phrases can't just be *"moves"* that you use. They have to be delivered in an authentic, honest, human way. Otherwise, it defeats the purpose of using them. This is really about finding words that feel natural and normal, but that you filtered out of your mind when you learned all the fancy ways to talk to business people. I'm suggesting that you strip away all the b.s. and be honest and direct with people. Yes, I want you to be savvy and sophisticated and, in the end, I want you to get more business. If you can do this in a more authentic way, you will stand out from others in your field, get more of the right conversations, find yourself avoiding business development activities less, and will feel better about yourself.

"When you lean psychologically or emotionally on people or toward them, it's a sure sign of insecurity. It makes others feel uncomfortable. They resent the weight you're laying on them, and they'll react by denying you. They don't like your self-indulgence, and your insecurity reminds them
of their own vulnerability; it rattles them.
... Remember, when your energy touches others, they subliminally
know if you're weak or strong — it affects how they see you."
— Stuart Wilde, Silent Power

The following are all phrases that have been tested in the text of prospecting emails, voice mails, phone conversations, and presentations. At first glance, they might appear "weak." As long as they are tied in with your ability to effectively communicate your unique value and deliver them from a place of confidence, they will help disarm people. Your prospects will be more apt to respond to and to open up to you with more information about what's really going on for them. Notice which ones you use (if any), as well as any strong emotional reactions you have to these phrases. They may run counter to all you have been taught to believe about how you are successful in the process of prospecting for new business.

· You probably don't know me.

· I'm pretty sure you have no idea who I am.

· I don't believe we've met.

· I don't think we know each other.

· You have no idea who the heck I am.

· This is a bit awkward for me, as I'm certain you don't know who I am.

· My intention is…

· Does that sound appropriate?

· If you are open…

· This is what I know… This is what I don't know…

· To best utilize your time and mine…

· What we have found works best…

· I am not sure if that is relevant to you.

· I'm not sure we can help you.

· I have no idea if any of this is relevant or of interest to you.

· I don't know if you're the person to talk to about this.

· I don't know who else might care about this issue.

· If you are open, the following works best for me…

· The next step would be.

· We are probably not the lowest price.

· If your top concern is price, we may not be a good fit, but if you are also considering… we may be a potential fit.

- At the end of the conversation, we will find out if we may have a potential fit.
- It is perfectly okay if we decide this is not going to be a good fit.
- We are not obligated to continue.
- Might...
- Possibly...
- Perhaps...
- Either way, I wish you the best.

"You must focus only on having conversations with well qualified prospects on an equal playing field. You must disarm them and be authentic and human enough to get the prospect to reveal their pain. It is then your job to communicate your value as concisely and meaningfully as possible. It will quickly become clear for both parties whether or not there is enough of a fit to talk further."

"Wishing you much success." or "I wish you the best" or "No matter what, I wish you the best." Always take the high road and wish people well, even if they don't want to talk with you further or work with you. Leave them with a positive, or at least neutral experience and memory of you and your organization.

Whenever I read this list of words and phrases out of context or imagine someone reading them for the first time, I worry that they will perceive these as counter to their sales goal which is to appear confident and strong and get the business. My intent is for you to get the business, if it's the right fit. You must first get the first meeting, and then the second meeting, and give yourself the best possible chance to get in the door and move the process forward in ways that allow you to be in control. These words and phrases need to be delivered with a certain level of clarity and confidence that still allows you to come from a position of equality. I believe you can talk like this, and do it strong and confidently, in a way that draws people to want to talk to you, to learn more, and to do business with you. I do not want you talking or appearing weak or wimpy.

Guiding Principles to Prospecting Communication

Here are a few examples of language that I've found will give you a better chance of getting a response and moving your process forward. They are more apt to disarm people and have them stay open to hear what you have to say. They have clear intent and next steps, and offer people an "out" which, in the end, gives you both a better chance of getting a truthful response and also gives you a better chance of getting a yes. Below you will find emails in three categories:

- Cold prospect
- When someone asks you to send information
- When you are at the beginning stages with a prospect or client and you have not heard back from them

The language can be used in face-to-face discussions, via phone, left on a voicemail, or in email. These will not cover all the scenarios you run into, but will give you an idea of key words and phrases we find most disarming and generate the most responses. They also give you an idea of the structure and flow of emails / communication I have found to be much more effective, especially with people who don't know you. Those who don't know you are most apt to quickly put up a wall and wonder who the heck you are. You also might want to consider how this approach to communicating could be relevant in your key client relationships, as well as when following up with referral sources.

Before we get into the specific language examples, here is the larger framework to consider the language fits in. The guiding principles to prospecting communication:

- Slow down, be clear, talk like a human being.
- Disarm up front.
- Quickly get to your point, be clear and specific about why you are calling, what you do, and who you do it for.
- Disarm them again, making no assumptions that they are interested or any of this information is relevant.
- Have a clear next step.
- Let them know you are OK either way (i.e.: if they are open to talk further, or not).

Effective Prospecting Example 1: Cold Prospect Email

Hi Tom. We have never met before. My name is Jody Hoffman and I am calling from Excell Research based in New York City.

Typically our firm works with clients who are looking for effective ways to better understand the drivers behind consumer behavior through market research. In turn our clients are then able to do things such as measure brand awareness and opinions, as well as effectiveness of advertising within the online community.

I have no idea if our company can be of assistance to you, however I thought I would call to see if you were open to a conversation. If this seems of interest or relevance to your company, the next step would be for us to schedule a brief, 5-10 minute exploratory conversation. If you're open to this, let me know. You can respond to me via phone at 800-***-5994, or you can respond to the email I sent you today with the same message.

If for some reason you're not open to talk, that's fine too. All that I ask is that you let me know either way. Have a good day.

Effective Prospecting Example 2: Cold Prospect Call

Hi Stuart, this is Lisa Tobin. First off, you don't know me. I work with a company here locally called Biotech Brand Solutions. Let me tell you quickly why I'm calling / writing.

We've been working very effectively with marketing managers at Bay Area biotech firms who are interested in building brand awareness and increasing sales. And, as a manufacturer, we've also helped these progressive-minded companies lower their overall production costs.

I don't have any idea if these topics are of interest to you or you're even the right person to talk with. I know you don't know me. I thought I'd call and see if you might be open to having a brief conversation to find out if any of what we do might be relevant.

Effective Prospecting Example 3: Cold Prospect Email

John,

Hi, This is Brad Gates. First off, I'm pretty sure you have no idea who the heck I am. I work with a company called Financial Images. We work with mid-sized brokerage firms based in Los Angeles that are growing rapidly. Clients we work with are highly image conscious and are open to new ideas about how to increase their name recognition and create presentation materials to help them win more business.

I have no idea if these are areas of interest to you. I know you don't know me from Adam. I thought I'd call and see if you might be open to having a brief conversation. At the end of the conversation, we'll have a good idea whether or not any of what we do might be relevant to you, or not.

Let me know if you're open to talk.

I recommend calling people and leaving a brief voice mail if you don't get them and then also sending an email with the same information. In the voice mail, I recommend you let them know you also sent them an email. It gives them two modes from which to respond to you. I know you want to talk with them live, but that is getting more and more difficult these days, which is why this approach is effective. If you can't get them live, sending an email and leaving a voicemail with the right message gives you the best possible chance to get a meeting or response.

Other Prospecting Scenarios
When a prospect asks you to "Send them some information."
When at all possible, take the time to have a conversation with your prospect and not just send them numbers and information. Once you send the numbers, or any other "stuff," you lose control. Don't assume that the person that requests the information is the person making the decision; often they are not. They have just been asked to gather information. Don't just immediately default to "their process." Clarify what "your process" is for these situations. And decide what steps you are willing to be flexible about / compromise on and what ones you are not.

It's important in these situations not to get into an ego battle. Even if you have a different process and can't or won't give your client what they want, it's important for them to feel heard, even understood. If you are then going to propose your next step, do not use a tone or language that discounts their perspective ("but" or "however" – i.e.: "I understand you want information, but that's not how we work.")

When your prospect or client has a different opinion or perspective on something (pricing, your value, the market, the world, themselves, etc.), your ego will want them to conform to your view of things, and their ego will want you to conform to theirs. The challenge here, if you are not on the same page, is to stay engaged even though you both have different perspectives on reality and what needs to happen. To maintain control and the high ground in conversation, it's important not to jump to any immediate conclusions that either they are right and you must default to their wishes, or that you are right and they are crazy and "screw 'em." This takes awareness and discipline. Rabbi Yehuda Halevi eloquently summarized this as the ability to **"Accommodate a competitive narrative."** By not resisting, you actually interrupt the pattern and don't give them anything to push back against. You've decided not to "dance" for them and yet also aren't pushing or forcing anything back their direction.

When they ask to send info. So, how do you push back on their request to send them something? Follow your process of not sending anything before first having a brief conversation.

Effective Declined Request for Information Example - 1

Hi Mark,

We received this email today from Karlene regarding a closed account survey.

To provide research that is meaningful, appropriate, and timely, what I find works best is for us to first have a ten minute conversation to identify your exact needs and budget requirements. Let me know if this works for you and when it would be convenient to talk.

Effective Declined Request for Information Example - 2

I have to be honest with you. I could send you a pile of information and samples, but in my experience, these materials end up on a desk / file somewhere and isn't the best use of your time or mine. I've found it most effective for us to have a brief conversation, either via phone or, ideally, face-to-face for each of us to quickly get an idea if there is – or isn't – any kind of fit or reason to talk further. If it turns out that there's a fit, then I would be happy to provide you with whatever tools and information you need.

My offer at this point is for you to invite me in to have a brief conversation. Are you open to that?

Here is a comment from a client of mine who faced this scenario. She did a great job respectfully pushing back at her prospect's request for her to send information.

"Then he asked me what I did. From there I took control of the process. I told him that though I know he must be curious about what we provide, I would rather ask him a few questions about his business so that I could talk about our company in a way that would be relevant to his business. He had no problem with that...and from there with me asking questions... he rambled on for a good 15-20 minutes."

Effective Declined Request for Information Example - 3

I can certainly send you an overview. However, we generally find it beneficial to talk briefly first. This way we can be sure to send you information that is relative to your needs. Benchmark Resources has a wide scope of services and we often find that when we

---

send "blanket overviews" you have to spend a lot of time weeding through material that doesn't apply to your business needs.

I recommend visiting our online website at www.XYZ.com which outlines our services and provides a recap of capabilities. This site also links you to our online resources, as well as our dedicated client site, and is a good source to get to familiarize yourself with the company.

If you still would like me to forward you some information prior to our discussion, I can certainly do this, but because we understand that our clients are busy (as are we), I just try and make sure that we make proper use of your time.

Would any of the following times work for you to schedule a conversation?

When You Have Not Heard Back From Someone...

This is the most fun one for me. If we could pull out one section of this book that is the closest thing to a magic pill (I know I said there were no magic pills here), this would be it. Everyone who is in sales, or is working directly with clients or prospective clients, has had a situation where someone is all of the sudden not responding to them. I call these stalled or lingering deals / situations. Moving these people back into your process or off the fence and out of your process is essential as lingering deals cost you time and money. This is a delicate process. We don't want to push people too hard and scare them off, and yet we want to move things forward.

These examples are all ones that got a response. The majority of the time, the response is yes, let's move forward to the next step (they just got busy or forgot, etc.). Occasionally you will get a response of, "No, not now." We have to be ok with any answer, as long as it is the truth. The goals here are:

- Get a response where we have not received one.
- Get the truth.
- If they are open to continue, get them to re-engage and agree on a next step.
- If they are not open to continue (at this time), close the loop (for now). This frees up headspace for you and creates a consequence for them to not be moving forward.

Effective Example 1

Dan,

We had talked and you said you were interested. I have not heard back from you.

Dan. I'm sure you have lots going on. I have not heard back from you so I am going to assume that now is not a good time to talk about our services and how they might be relevant to your stated concern about business growth this fiscal year.

If I'm mistaken and you want to talk, let's schedule some time next week for an exploratory phone call. Otherwise, I won't bug you further and wish you nothing but the best.

Tim

Notice the key elements of the above email: data (no emotion, just stating the facts) and giving him an out (almost daring him to go away, taking the high road).

Response

Tim,

You're right; things have been very hectic lately. I would like to hear more about the programs that you offer and if Tuesday March 13th is good for you then we can get together over the phone. I would like to talk around 1pm, Chicago time, but if you prefer a different time I'm flexible. Thanks, and I look forward to talking to you.

Dan

Effective Example 2

Chris,

I'm sure you have lots going on. I have not heard back from you so am going to assume that now is not a good time to talk about how our approach to Internet marketing could increase the Lightquest's online sales.

If I'm mistaken and you want to talk, let's schedule some time next week to continue our conversation or get started. Otherwise, I won't bug you further and wish you nothing but the best.

Steve

Notice the willingness to walk away. By stating, respectfully and without emotion (i.e.: annoyance), that you're going away, you give them the chance to say "No, don't go." This is often the only way to get someone's attention. It has to be done in the right way. If done correctly (like all of these examples), you will get a response in situations where you could not previously get the person to call or email you back.

Response

Steve, Sorry, I flew to New York on Friday and have been away. The answer is that I am open. I want to hear the suggestion our PR company has come up with. I have not ruled anything out yet. Let's stay in touch. I am back in town next week.

thx Chris

Effective Example 3

Rob,

The last time we talked you mentioned you were interested in getting together to talk further and have me meet with some of your new Financial Planners. Before doing that you wanted to discuss with your branch manager first. Since we last spoke, I sent you an email at the end of August and I have not heard from you.

I'm going to assume that something has changed and this is not of interest to you at this time. If I'm mistaken, let me know. I'd be happy to schedule a time to talk further with you. I'll assume we are done for now, and wish you nothing but the best. If at any point in the near future you'd like to talk, feel free to email or call at 203-***-1093.

Take care, Teri

See how she takes the high road? If they are open to talk now, a response will come. Even if now isn't the right time, this email leaves a positive emotional tag in the prospect's brain. They will remember the professionally and non-pushy way that Teri communicated. It may lead to business now, and if not now, it will lead to being considered for future opportunities. Remember, we are first selling for the now and looking for immediate opportunities. But, we are also planting seeds for the future. How we handle these situations is a chance to differentiate ourselves from the competition — talking, acting differently than anyone else. While being clear and direct and respectful.

Response

Teri,

Actually I am having my follow up meeting with my Manager on Wednesday at 10:00AM. Sorry about the delay, but the wheels around here grind very slowly. I don't know what will come from it, but I am planning to call you later that day.

Each of these received a response in a situation where they were not previously getting a response. I cannot say that they all led to business. I can say that they all moved the process forward to the next step. If you have any scenarios where things are stalled and you can't get a response, consider adopting this approach. You can customize the details to make them relevant to your situation. The more you read these examples, the more you get a sense of the underlying structure and guiding principles that make them different and subsequently effective.

Below is a note from one of my business partners who was working with clients on these "detachment / I'm going away" emails.

"Most business and sales professionals struggle with attachment — they can't let go. Being attached to deals that are dead and they can't seem to let go because "they're a big company and there could be lots of potential there" even though they haven't returned my 50 calls and emails. "I'm not comfortable saying that I'm going away." What has been helpful is talking through the going away emails with them and having them draft those with my feedback and sending them out. They all felt that saying they were going away was forever and that's not the case. Very simple and yet they struggle with it."

Even if your "old way" works ok for you, I'm suggesting that it's inefficient. You may very well be putting yourself in a compromising position (however subtle) and are wasting time on things that are going nowhere. You may also be missing opportunities to make a deeper connection with the right client. Everything that I'm suggesting is designed to help you to be more efficient and effective at getting more of the right kinds of conversations with more of the right kinds of clients. Feel free to create your own version of these scripts, and see how they work for you.

Key Reminders:

- The goal is for your words NOT to sound eager or needy for your clients' business. Even if you do get the business later, it's hard to negotiate from a position of equality when you start the relationship this way.

- Remember your time is as valuable as theirs. They have challenges and you have solutions. You are reaching out to see if there is any kind of a fit. Stop thanking people for their time (i.e.: "Thank you for taking a few minutes to speak with me today"). If you want to have more control in sales and negotiations, you need to stop this.

- No begging. "Please" is a begging, pleading word. Again, I know you were taught to say please as a child. As a high level professional and adult it is seldom needed or even appropriate. Especially with people that you don't know and are not currently doing business with. If you want to be on equal ground with prospects and key clients, eliminate the word **please**.

- People are busy. Make your communication short, sweet, and to the point.

UPFRONT FRAME FOR PROSPECTING CONVERSATIONS

Preview Points:

- Create a framework around every conversation and increase your chances for getting more useful, truthful information.
- Create a process where you are in control without appearing to be controlling. Speak with a focused, casual effortlessness.
- Prepare yourself for every possible question and scenario so nothing surprises you or throws you off your game.

"The prospect has his ego involved from the start as you begin to talk. Ego is pure emotion. And most of the time, it's rooted in FEAR. That fear comes in several different areas: fear that you will do something to hurt him (psychologically), fear that you will expose his previous wrongs, fear that he will make the wrong decision, fear that by opening up to you, you will destroy his pride and dignity. It is impossible to solve an emotional problem intellectually. The part most salespeople miss is how emotional the initial part of the sales process is."
— Bill Caskey, Same Game, New Rules,

When meeting, either face-to-face or via phone, with prospects, there is one opportunity to create an Upfront Framework for your conversation. This framework is designed to help keep you in control, put others at ease so they will share more information with you, and waste less time.

New business opportunities unfold as a series of moments. Some of these moments are more pivotal than others. You only get one chance in each moment; to start a meeting in the right way, to be in the proper mindset, to ask or be able to answer a difficult question, and in turn, get someone's attention and concisely communicate your intent as well as who you are and what's unique about your organization. You only get one chance to find out about people's current business problems, opportunities, and what they are open to.

People like to know what's coming next and where they stand. Reviewing where we are in the sales process at each step keeps everyone clear. Letting them know what to expect next keeps them calm.

In order to ensure the best possible outcome, there are a number of reminders to consider prior to an initial email, phone call, or next step in an important conversation with a client.

- Clarify Intent. Be clear with people why you are writing, calling, or meeting. Even if you think they know, don't assume that's the case. Make sure everyone understands where you are coming from and that there is agreement about what is to happen.

- Authenticity. Be human, personable (but not fake), honest, and direct. Show up naturally curious, interested, and ready to listen. Be normal. No need to put on a mask, try too hard, get too excited, etc.

- Being ok with "not knowing" what it is you don't know (i.e.: What they are open to, If you are a good fit for them, etc.).

- Detachment. Be prepared and fully engaged in your conversations. In that moment, don't spend energy worrying about whether or not this is going to lead to new business.

- Shut up. Learn when and how to use silence appropriately. Sometimes, pausing or just not talking can be the best thing you can do.

- Know your value. Be able to clearly articulate why people work with you, what kind of opportunities you're looking to attract, and who you are interested in doing business with.

- Slow down. Take your time when preparing, talking, and asking questions. Don't move too quickly, especially if you're nervous.

> *"At the end of the day, having high intent makes you feel good about who you are and how you are going about your business."*

As you are building out the structure for your conversations, here is a guide to what you're up against. In the end, your job is to facilitate a process, starting with your Upfront Framework, that relaxes people and gets them to tell you the truth. Many in business will naturally default to lying, withholding, focusing on price, trying to get free information, and dictating next steps. This is not because they are bad people, it's just what people do.

Their Process

- Lie or withhold information
- Use only rational, logical filters
- Get free information and consulting
- Focus primarily on price
- Prospect controls when, where
- Voicemail hell — seller is last to know

Your Process

- Upfront Frame for every conversation
- Uncovering their pains, opportunities, what they are open to
- Analyzing the economics of their pain, opportunities
- Negotiating the process for moving forward
- Presentation of final solutions

(Original introduction to the "Their Process vs. Your Process" concept first introduced to me by Bill Caskey of Caskey Achievement Strategies)

Operating with High Intent

"Sales" and "High intent" are seldom viewed as synonymous. When I ask a workshop audience to give me their initial reactions to the word "sales," "high-intent" is never on the list. Usually the first words I hear are slimy, pushy, greedy, selfish. This is where the opportunity for differentiation lies.

I had lunch recently with a friend who is an entrepreneur and runs free seminars, providing useful information for anyone who is interested in his topic. People are always skeptical of anything that's free. They keep waiting for him to ask for their credit card number or for the hard sell to come. But it never comes. Now, he does give them an opportunity to follow up with a meeting at a later date. He also gives them a chance to state their interest in learning more about what his company does and how it might be relevant or have an impact on their business. But, no hard sell. Providing value. No strings attached. Providing an opportunity, for those that are open to it and interested, for more information and a next step, but never any coercion or uncomfortable sales pressure.

Intent is a challenge, even for the most high-minded of us. It is hard not to be attached to the money, the deal, the accolades, the win, the score, and the victory. I am all about winning, and what I have found is that most professionals actually limit opportunities for winning new business while pushing to make it happen. This happens when your intent is too pushy, too selfish, and you get too attached to the deal. When you are worrying more about winning and making money than you are about solving the client's problem and genuinely wanting to help them find the best solution, your winning percentage for long-term, profitable new business will significantly decrease.

Ego, fear, and greed will lead you to negotiate and communicate with prospects from a place of what I call "low intent." This solely transactional motive is all about getting the deal at any cost. This approach is manipulative, attached to one outcome only, fearful of losing, and grounded in a place of weakness. You cannot find more ideal clients that will be with you for life, pay their bills on time, and be a pleasure to work with from a place of low intent.

High intent comes from making "no" acceptable at each step of the way, asking very pointed and specific questions, being curious and genuine, seeking the truth, and caring about solving the prospect's problem (without caring more than they do).

> "If you combine the right intent with a clear and effective process, you will make quantum leaps in results."

If you're coming from the place of high intent, your mind is clear. Of course you want to close the deal, but never more than the other party wants their problem solved. And from a place of high intent, you are, in the end, ok with "no" if it is clear there is not a good fit, or they are not open to working with you. This is the hardest concept for most driven professionals to swallow and practice. Again, I'm not suggesting you not care. I am saying that most of us hold on too long and push too hard when a deal is already dead. I want you to close more deals, make more money, and help more people. There is a way to accomplish this that uses optimal amounts of your energy, lets the prospect opt in to a process that you control, and allows everyone the best possible chance to get their needs met.

These *High Intent* conversations lead to more of the right kinds of new clients and deeper relationships with your current ones.

When you are preparing for a meeting, your first step should be to ask yourself, *"What is my intent for this conversation?"* Most everyone hates to be sold, doesn't like being out of control, and gets uncomfortable if they don't know what to expect next. Busy professionals, especially, hate wasting their valuable time.

In order to get the prospect to share openly what's going on, you need to first be clear about what they can expect. You let them know the intent (i.e.: purpose) of this meeting / email / phone call, and what you intend to accomplish, share, and ask. Also ask them what they would like to accomplish. And, at the risk of being overly specific, clarify your agreements (i.e.: how much time have we committed for this conversation) and what will be next (i.e.: what our options are for next steps at the end of the meeting). This is all designed to create what I call a safe and highly structured "container" to operate within. Once you have all the structure set up and out of the way, you and your prospect are free to have an in-depth, meaningful, human conversation. I am interested in eliminating all the little things that might be on the prospect's mind that could keep them from being fully present and sharing openly with me.

In an initial conversation the simple goal is to give your prospect an idea of who you are, what you do, and why people hire you. To ask them some questions, and be open to answering any questions they have of you. You have done this enough to know that 90% of the time, you have a pretty good idea within a few minutes if you might have a fit and if it's a good use of your time to continue talking. You want to be equally respectful of both their time and yours. The more clear and honest you are with people right up front, the more likely they are to return your honesty in kind. This is not guaranteed, but will give you the best chance to have a more thoughtful, productive conversation.

The clarity and quality of this interaction sets the tone for everything to come. Do not underestimate the importance of how every one of your conversations begins. In *Blink*, Malcolm Gladwell writes about doctors who were the least likely to be sued. One of the elements that proved most important was taking the time to orient their patients about what to expect during their appointment or procedure. Often people go into an important new business conversation or negotiation with little or no plan. They just "wing it," hoping for the best.

> *"They were more likely to make orienting comments, such as "First I'll examine you, and then we will talk the problem over" or "I will leave time for your questions" - which help patients get a sense of what the visit is supposed to accomplish and when they ought to ask questions. They were more likely to engage in active listening, saying such things as "Go on, tell me more about that" and they were far more likely to laugh and be funny during the visit... The difference was entirely in how they talked to their patients."*
> — Malcolm Gladwell, Blink

Another important theme in creating an effective framework or structure to your prospecting conversations is the concept of not moving too fast. It's one of the topics in this program that inspires a "What, are you nuts!?" look from many top earning salespeople and high-profile business professionals. They want to "strike while the iron is hot" and "always be closing." I once told a struggling VP of Sales for a professional services firm that instead of speeding up I thought he actually needed to slow down. I thought he was throwing so much unfocused and inefficient energy toward trying to get new business (so as not to get fired) that he was much less effective than he could have been and needed to be. He thought I was crazy. And two months later, he got fired. Sometimes its hard to slow things down when you're caught in a whirlwind of what I call "just doing what you have always done that worked pretty well up until now."

Take a look at how world-class track coach John Smith describes how to run a race.

> "Many people believe that in order to win a race, you have to be the first one out of the blocks," says Smith. "They're wrong. The most important thing is to execute a balanced start. The first step sets up every step that follows. If you're the slightest bit overextended, you have to rebalance yourself -- which displaces energy and sacrifices time. But if you're balanced properly, you're prepared to handle the choreography that will allow you to win."

Every conversation in your new client engagement process should begin with you, the professional expert, FRAMING the conversation. Although we mentioned this a couple of paragraphs earlier it bears repeating. Framing the conversation includes things such as: giving everyone an overview of your understanding of why you're talking, what the intent is for the conversation, basic details of what to expect, how much time is allotted, and what the options will be at the end of the conversation. In many ways, these reminders are all about getting "back to basics." It is easy to get caught up in so many other details and move quickly ahead to what you want to tell the prospect that you can forget about the basics of creating a clear Upfront Framework first.

When you start by framing the conversation, you establish three things.

- You are in control (without being controlling).
- Your intent for a transparent and truthful conversation.
- You are OK with any outcome: yes let's move forward —or- no, let's not.

The art of *framing* your conversation makes you appear casual, and friendly, while at the same time maintaining an underlying structure. You are clear about the purpose and intent of every interaction. You show confidence and are in control, while also being flexible, humble, and open minded within your structured approach. The better you are at executing this approach, the more of a chance you will have of getting the truth from your prospects and clients in a short period of time.

I was working with a client around just this issue. She has been working with me for a couple of years, yet got a little lazy lately with a couple of high level prospecting conversations. For example, she launched into her pitch and forgot to set the stage with a framework (i.e.: why we're talking, what she's interested in sharing as well as asking, what comes at the end, etc.). Her client was a bit confused and the whole call was very unfocused. I reminded her that the upfront frame is as much for her as it is for her client. Here's where the resistance comes in. The ego within your mind wants you to trust your assumption that the other person knows why you're meeting. The ego hates to risk stating the obvious. It doesn't want the other person to think, "Duh! No kidding! Of course!"

I believe you are much better off assuming that no one is certain about the intent of the meeting. You have to continuously start over, even in mid-process, with multiple conversations, restate your intent, and clarify mutual expectations. This ensures you have a focused, productive conversation that also happens to establish your capability, strength, and equality with your prospect or client.

Notice any assumptions you make about what they think or know and any fear you have about possible awkwardness in using some version of an upfront frame. I have never once had a prospect in my own business or with one of my clients respond to an attempt at an Upfront Frame with a negative or uncooperative comment. It's kind of a no brainer, really, if you can get past your ego's fear of looking like a moron. Ego hates what it would call "stating the obvious." You are not a moron. You are a smart, thoughtful person that is looking for the best way to use both your prospect's and your own time. You have experience with what's effective and what wastes time. You are risking stating the obvious, and have good reason for doing so. Anyone who reacts poorly to that is obviously not someone you would want as a client anyway. So, follow the process and always frame your conversation up front in some way.

Effective Upfront Frame Samples – How to start a meeting

* Disclaimer: When starting a meeting, my intent is always to come across as casual and non-scripted as possible, while also adhering to some form of an upfront frame that sets the structure for the conversation. These examples might seem a little "stiff." They are not designed to be recited or read like a monologue. I trust you will find your way to integrate some of this language and intent into your own style and approach.

Sample Upfront Framework 1: New Prospect
My intent for this call is to give you a better sense of what we do, how we think, and why people hire us. I also want to find out a little more about your organization, what's working, what's not, as well as better understand your role. At the end of our scheduled 30 minutes, we should have a good idea if we have any reason to talk further. If so, we can discuss what a next step would look like. If not, then neither of us will have wasted much time. Does that sound fair?

Sample Upfront Framework 2: New Prospect
What I'd like to do is ask you some questions about your organization and some of the challenges you have. And for you to feel free to ask about us and what we do. At the end of our time today, we can decide if there is any reason to talk further. If there is, we can discuss where we go next. If not, that's fine. Are you ok with that?

Sample Upfront Framework 3: Past/Current Client
What I thought we would do today first is recap our history together. Then, I'd like to ask you a few questions about what prompted you to invite me in today. Then, I'll open up for any questions you might have or to discuss any lingering issues.

At the end, we should both have a good sense if it makes sense to talk further. If we both agree it does, then we can discuss the next steps. And if either of us thinks there's not a fit here and no reason to talk further, that's fine too. I'll be on my way and neither of us has wasted much time. Does that seem appropriate?

In first meetings, there is often a compulsion to show the prospect too much. Be aware of this urge. Ask questions, probe, and gather information. Talk less — if you're talking more than them, you're dead. Notice any attachment to the outcome of the meeting. Be curiously interested in the people across from you and whether or not you might be able to help them. Most of all, have fun; be human.

Your job is to have conversations with qualified prospects on an equal playing field, disarm them enough, and be human enough to give yourself an opportunity to hear them reveal their pain. Communicate your value in a concise, relevant, and meaningful way and then together decide if there is any kind of fit or reason to talk further. That's it.

If you have enough of these conversations, are unattached, are being yourself, and follow your plan, you will significantly increase your results.

Reminder: You & Your Time Are Valuable

As you are having conversations with new prospects, past clients, and current clients, keep in mind that you have a short period of time to give and receive a lot of substantive information. The more prepared you are and the better you frame your conversation, the quicker and more efficiently you can get into a meaningful dialogue. People will respect and appreciate this approach. All this doesn't mean you can't also be conversational and human, of course. That being said, your job is to help them understand the value of the service you offer, in the context of their world (what's working for them, what's not work, what's important to them, etc.), not your world. By focusing on qualifying the opportunity rather than just trying to close a sale, you create an environment of trust. Instead of being part of the problem and overwhelming prospects with massive PowerPoints and data, we learn to focus on the issues at hand and to help the prospect understand the extent of the problem and how we might be able to help them.

Key Reminders:

- Being detached from the outcome helps you focus on getting the truth.

- Be authentically curious about better understanding your client's issues, opportunities, and whether or not you can help them.

- The more *emotional* and *personal* you can get, the better chance you will have at helping others solve their problems.

- Have a *qualification mindset* for every call. Remember you are interviewing them for fit as much as they are you. Notice when you're just happy to get an appointment and have someone talk to you.

- Act normal. Although you are executing a process that has structure and scripts, your job is to be *normal*, matter of fact, and conversational. Notice when you sound or your delivery feels forced.

CURIOSITY &
KEY QUESTIONS

Preview Points:

- You can't fake asking good questions or being authentically curious and interested.

- Not knowing is perfectly OK and often puts you in a position of strength, despite what you might think.

- The more excited and pumped up you are, the less you're able to listen effectively.

Curiosity Can't Be Faked

Be curious and obsessed with finding the truth. Ask good questions. Actually listen to the answers.

As a professional responsible for getting new business, you should be obsessed with one thing: The Truth. Nothing else is really important. In a typical selling relationship you often have critical information withheld or even get lied to. The only way to get the truth about your prospect's situation is to ask in a way where they understand your intent and that it's safe for them to give you all the information you need. I believe when you ask thoughtful, meaningful, well-crafted questions that you will uncover more opportunities to solve people's problems, get more clients, and subsequently make more money. Your questions, ability to listen, and genuineness throughout the process will help differentiate you from the competition.

Think about the quality of a recent conversation with a prospective new client. Did you ask thoughtful and sometimes challenging questions? Did you truly listen to the answers? Did you have some sort of structure to your conversation (i.e.: how you started it, what you asked, how you wrapped it up and clarified the next step)?

Controlling Adrenaline

The more excited or nervous you are, the less you are able to listen. I'm sure you have your own tricks for calming down and staying focused during stressful encounters. When your heart is pumping and you're feeling excited (or scared), you are able to give information (output), but struggle to take it in, process it, and integrate it into your responses spontaneously (input, input-output). By showing up and appearing calm with a new prospect, you send a message to the prospect that you are not a threat and are not needy of their business. Too often people show up looking, acting, and talking a bit like a predator stalking its prey. They are selling hard, pushing, and even showing off. You may not act like this, but I'm sure you've seen professionals who do. On the flipside, sometimes professionals who are responsible for developing new business but do not consider themselves salespeople show up too passive, low-key, and aloof (at least in appearance).

The key is to find an optimal middle place. When I think about what that means for me when I am meeting with a big, new prospect, I want to be confident, clear, and have a good sense of my value. I also, at some level, want to not really care whether I get their business or not. I am interested in helping them uncover their problems and opportunities and finding out if we might have a good fit for working together. I am not

"Be direct and honest with clients and prospects about what you KNOW and what you DON'T KNOW. This is a great starting point for any strong, radically honest and productive dialogue."

particularly worried about the outcome. If I am, I must fake it. I am most interested in having productive, meaningful conversations. I trust that in the end, this will lead to plenty of the right kinds of business for me and my organization. Despite my efforts to find evidence to the contrary, this approach has always successfully worked in my favor.

What I Know, What I Don't Know

Too many people are trying way too hard to be someone they think others want them to be. Business-speak, buzzwords, posturing, and fake sincerity are rampant at work — and especially in sales. The greatest asset you have in sales situations is you. Some are going to like you and your approach and want to work with you. Some are not. The clearer you communicate the following things to potential and current clients, the better off you will be.

- Who you are.
- How you work.
- What you believe.
- What you and your company are good at.
- What you and your company are not as good at or don't focus on.
- Who you want to work with, find to be the best fit.
- Who you don't want to work with, don't find to be a good fit.

Be human. Be honest. Don't b.s. people. They see right through it. If you don't know an answer, say you don't know. You don't have to have all the answers. People find candor, clarity, and humility quite refreshing — especially in business and sales.

The framework of "What I know" and "What I don't know" can be an effective way to disarm a client and still come from a position of strength. This also sets up the important questions that you need to learn the answers to.

Things you know are irrefutable facts, or data. You might say you "I know we are a great fit" to a client if you are just meeting them. You might think this from your perspective, but you do not really know this to be true. Be direct and clear with yourself and with the others about what you don't know. There is nothing wrong with not knowing. These statements, if done in a clear and confident tone (not apologetic and weak), can actually reinforce your position of strength and equality. Talking like this will also differentiate you from the competition because no one else is talking like this.

To be done effectively, the details of an exercise like "What I know / What I don't know" need to be specifically custom to your situation. There will obviously be detailed questions you have that are not represented below. This template is designed to get you thinking in this way. Use it in any way you like to help guide your key questions and overall process with new prospective clients. I have filled a few examples just to give you an idea of the kinds of things you could include. There are no real limits or boundaries to what goes in this list of what you know and don't know. Make it your own based on your real-time situations.

What I Know
- You have told me you are in a hurry
- We worked with you on a project two years ago
- You say your budget is $20,000
- You say an important client relationship is on the line for you
- You want a proposal by end of day Friday

What I Don't Know

- Who else has a stake in this getting solved
- Why you are considering us again now
- How you decided on that figure
- What's it worth to save them and keep them happy
- If you are open to have a conversation first

> *"In our culture we've been conditioned to look at not knowing as something unacceptable and bad; it's some kind of failure."*
> — William Arntz, Betsy Chasse, Mark Vicente,
> What the Bleep Do We Know!?

Maybe you think you can help your prospect with their big project because you've done similar projects before and it seems like a "no brainer" to you. That being the case, there are always things (in your first couple of conversations) that you don't know: the project details, timelines, who else they are talking to, who else is involved in this decision, who else has a stake in getting this project done on time, etc. So, as much as you are confident in yourself and your company's ability to deliver, it's important to throw in a word here and there that creates "space" so you don't sound too assumptive, overly eager, or over-confident (even boastful). You can be strong in how you show up, and talk about your competence, experience, and perspective. At the same time, especially early on in your process, it's important to not get too far ahead of your client, not to sell too hard and too fast, or you will trigger resistance. Or worse yet, you will get them so excited that they move too quickly in their process and get caught up in the moment with you, only to pull back later. Here are a few words that create space and minimize resistance:

· Might	· Not sure	· Open to
· Could	· Possibly	· No idea

Key Questions

Q: What do people in sales, business most struggle with?
A: " They avoid asking the tough questions and having a real conversation ...
that helps truly qualify the opportunity. They avoid because this might
lead to a "no" in just a few minutes. They want to keep hope alive as long
as possible. On top of that, most salespeople are not prepared in advance,
they have no concept of what questions they will ask, or what they want to
leave the room with, or what their next step is. This is what they struggle
with: fear. Fear comes from being unprepared, from the unknown."

— Bill Crouch, National Sales Director

There is nothing more important in the process of selling and serving clients than asking good questions. I'm sure there have been thousands of books written on the subject. It's one thing to be curious and ask questions, it's another to ask the right questions, at the right time. There are some questions we are comfortable with and easily ask all the time. There are other questions that we think about, but don't ask. Why is that? Because we are uncomfortable. We don't want to put anyone on the spot, appear rude, or are afraid of the answer. In order to close more deals, you have to say things that your emotional brain will fear might jeopardize the deal and risk making someone mad. It has been my experience that it's actually more risky to NOT ask these questions. If you don't have certain information early on in your process, you risk wasting a lot of time and energy on something that has a very small chance of ever becoming new business.

> *"Asking questions opens the door to the unknown. You have to be willing to receive an answer you don't agree with or don't want to hear. It takes courage to ask questions."*

"The ultimate solutions to problems are rational, the process of finding them is not."
—John O'Keefe, Business Beyond the Box

Before we go further, create a list of key questions you always want to have answers to from a prospect before doing a presentation / proposal. Notice which ones are easiest for you to ask and get answers to and which ones feel slightly uncomfortable and are hard at times to get answered.

Key Questions to Ask

_____

_____

_____

_____

In a little bit you will have a chance to check these out against some of the questions that I find most helpful and effective. What I'm most interested in is that next, most uncomfortable question that needs to be asked. It needs to be asked but you are afraid to ask, or you are just not sure how to ask it, and so you give up and don't bring it up. This is usually the question that has the most potential to _quickly_ spin a prospect out of your process (i.e.: not a good fit or worth pursuing further). Subsequently, it also has the best chance to deepen your dialogue and _spin_ them further into your new client engagement process. It takes courage to risk more quickly _spinning_ someone into or out of your engagement process. Most people like to hold onto a prospect as long as they can, "hoping" that something will happen, even if they know in their heart and mind that they are not a good fit or are not ready to make a change at this time.

The key questions listed below can be delivered in written or spoken form. Some of the questions need an intro or buffer of some kind before you launch into them. The important thing is not walking through this list, but ensuring that you identify the key questions that are essential to get answered during your process. Be honest with yourself about the ones you are most comfortable and uncomfortable asking. It is essential that you understand the intent and reasoning behind asking each of these questions. There must be a reason for asking each question, besides you wanting to sell them something, right? Asking a certain question will help you, and them, better understand important information designed to determine if you really can help them or not. We all have been in situations where we didn't ask some of these questions, went far down the path of our engagement process, and then got blind sided when the deal fell through or the client changed their tune.

All of these questions are designed to better understand the prospect's issues, current situation, compelling reason to change, and whether or not you are a good fit to help them at this time. The sooner you can do that, the less time you will waste on bad prospects or chasing bad deals, and the more time you will spend on good prospects and getting good business. Sounds simple. We all want that, right? And yet, there are questions you are not asking in your new client engagement process and with new projects from existing clients. Here are a few of the questions I find important to ask or get answered in some fashion that many business professionals forget about or get afraid to bring up.

> *"There are no easy answers... mostly just questions and conversations and creativity."*
> — David Whyte

Key Questions

- Why are we talking now? Why have you agreed to invite me in to talk?
- Why is this a good time to be talking? Is there any reason why now might not be a good time?
- What did you like about what you heard / read about us and the work we do?
- Related to... , what is currently working well?
- Related to... , what is currently not working as well as you would like?
- Related to... , what matters most to you?
- Is there anyone else who cares about this?
- Why change? Why not keep doing what you have been doing?
- What's the cost of this problem?
- Is there any urgency around the timing for making a decision?
- What are the steps, factors, and priorities guiding your decision making process?
- Are you talking to other companies about this as well?

"People do not like being skeptical – they want to like and be liked and believe the customer is that great person who is going to buy. They do not ask tough enough questions because they fear losing the opportunity. In the end, they come across as a sales person, regurgitating the marketing info that was taught to them instead of simply holding a conversation."
— Jacqueline Rosales, Vice President of Business Development

I have a client I've been working with for a couple of years now. Each person on the business development / project development team has their own approach with new prospects and new opportunities with existing clients. That being said, there is a core list of things they know they must understand early on in the process that will help them and their clients more quickly decide if they should move forward or not. They are uncompromising with their focus on getting answers to these questions. They have sold the old way, and got tired of wasting time and energy on projects that went nowhere and on dead end prospects that talked a good game, but didn't come through. They are diligent, focused, and respectfully uncompromising with their key questions that must be answered within the first two calls / meetings related to a new piece of potential business. Here is a sample of their list. You will find similarities to my list above. The repetition is on purpose. What might yours look like?

Questions to Determine if There is a Next Step with a Prospect

from a Current Client

- Why are you considering a change?
- Why did you reach out to engage in a conversation with us?
- Business volume, project size, kinds of work done, etc.?
- Urgency around and timing for making a decision?
- Important factors in your decision making process for working with a new partner?
- What's the cost of this problem (or not getting it solved) to you?
- We have a bit of a different process than you might be used to for finding out if we are a going to be a good fit. Are you open to being flexible with your process?

> · Who else in the organization cares about these issues?
> · Pricing/budget/expectations?

"You have to be incredibly curious and want to know why and how, not just whether or not," Rhein says. "Every answer they give you should lead you to another open-ended question: How did you do that? How did you respond to that? What else?" Find out what they really mean. People tend to rely heavily on assumptions to communicate."
— Barry Rhein, Fast Company Magazine August 2000,
Article by Cheryl Dahle

Sometimes when I am doing real-time deal coaching with clients, I will ask them, "If there were no rules, no boundaries, and you could ask anything you wanted and be radically direct and honest, what else might you want to ask?" This is a useful exercise to go through. The key is to be human, detached, unemotional, and authentically curious. Now, some of the things you write down that you'd like to ask, you can't because your clients will get defensive or just not tell you the truth. Most of the questions you come up with in this exercise are exactly the right questions to ask. I am amazed at how often we don't ask these key questions, with the highest intent, in a direct and thoughtful way.

Here are the answers a couple of my clients came up with when working through this exercise.

- "I'd like to ask a lot of them what holds them back from having a bigger plan and why they seem hesitant to break out of the ordinary. Why some of them show interest but just don't buy."

- "I am curious who else they do business with. What makes those consistent suppliers stand out or their product stand out. I'd like to ask them details about how their business operates that will help me get them talking about specifics that I can actually apply to improve what we do for them."

- "I want to know why they chose someone else on the last project we bid on with them. What those people had that we didn't and why they didn't choose us. We can learn from this."

Consider that you actually can ask these things. I believe you are obligated to ask them. If you are not asking, there is a good chance you are wasting your prospect's and your time. No one is going to yell at you for asking. If, for some reason, they do, then they probably aren't a good prospective client, now are they?

"Most people don't lie intentionally, but unless you really probe, you're not asking them to go beyond the pat answers they have rehearsed. That means you'll always get the positive data, but you're not getting the full story."
— Barry Rhein, Fast Company Magazine August 2000,
Article by Cheryl Dahle

Find a Prospect's Compelling Reason to Change Before Presenting Solutions.

I have witnessed countless scenarios where people have presented specific solutions, prepared a complex proposal, and even negotiated financial details and talked about money before they asked, or received an answer, to the question of client's compelling reason to change. Directly or indirectly asking about and uncovering things such as:

- "Why now?"
- "Why not wait?"
- "Why not just keep doing what you're doing?"
- "Why us?"

- "What's the cost of that (issue to be solved / opportunity to capitalize on)?"
- "Why does this matter to YOU?"
- "What have you heard from us that is compelling enough for you to consider such a change / investment?"

When I ask new clients or workshop participants why a prospect is considering them for a project, they almost always say, *"We think it's because…"* Then I ask if they have asked the prospect why they are considering them and what's compelling about the idea of working with them based on what they have seen and heard to date. And they usually say no. Why don't we ask this question? We don't ask because we are afraid of rejection, afraid they won't tell us what we want to hear, afraid they won't have any answers at all, and afraid we might look stupid.

I have seen people in new business development waste five, ten, or even twenty hours working on fancy presentations and proposals that end up going nowhere because they didn't ask some basic questions during the first few meetings. I understand that sometimes it's important to give presentations and submit proposals without having every detail. That being said, there are fundamental questions that must be answered before we move deeper into our process. If the prospect can't give you an authentic and compelling reason why they are considering you for a project or doing the project at all, then something is wrong. That's the time to circle the wagons and have a different conversation, or decide to bow out gracefully and move on.

Your time is valuable. Respect yourself and your process. Your prospect's time is valuable, too. Respect them enough to not want to waste their time. Find out their compelling reasons to change before moving too far into the process and presenting final solutions.

Key Questions for Ending a Prospect Meeting

I've found it useful to clarify perceptions through a "Plus/ Delta" assessment, a variation on the "Plus/Minus" measure, at the end of every meeting. The "Plus" involves asking about what worked, what the client and you like about what's been discussed, etc. The "Delta" is to uncover what's not working, what has not been addressed, what concerns or unknowns are still lingering, etc. Many people are uncomfortable with this process. They may feel its egotistical or asking people to state the obvious. They may also prefer to focus on the positive aspects of the relationship and avoid its shortcomings. The thing is, if there are questions and concerns, you need to know about them. You can't speak to them and try and solve them if you don't know they exist. It seems so easy, yet I see most every-one in business and sales do a poor job of this.

There is a simple, two-part question most people in sales fail to ask at the end of each client meeting.

---

1. What Worked?

- "What was compelling, interesting, and relevant about our conversation?"

- "What is it about what you've heard so far that is compelling, interesting, and on target?"

- "What do you like about what you've heard?"

- "Reasons that it makes sense to consider moving to the next step?"

- "Reasons why it might make sense to consider working together?"

---

2. What didn't work?

- "What wasn't compelling, interesting or relevant?"
- "Anything you were hoping to hear that I didn't address?"
- "Reasons why it doesn't make sense to work together"
- "What lingering questions and concerns do you still have?"

There are many forms of these questions. What's most important is that you ask them consistently as part of your process. It is equally important that you are also answering the same questions yourself. Ideally you are doing this as a part of your conversation review with your prospect. If nothing else, you are at least running through your answers to these questions in your head or discussing them during your internal meetings about particular new prospects. Remember that this is a two-way street. You are both interviewing each other and deciding if you have a good fit. We often don't ask these questions because we're afraid of hearing what didn't work for them, what they are concerned about, and what they still aren't clear about or sold on. A part of us doesn't want to hear what we didn't do a good job of or what someone doesn't like. We're also afraid of silence, of them not telling us, not cooperating, or thinking it's odd or inappropriate for us to ask these questions.

If you are uncomfortable asking these questions, you can always frame them by sharing why you find it's important to ask them. Sometimes I say something like, "What I find is helpful at the end of these meetings is to do a quick plus/delta to do a review of where we are. If we can all share something about what we like so far about what we've heard and any lingering questions or concerns, we can then decide what we'd like to happen next. So, if you're open to it, I'd like to go around the table and I'll record everyone's responses. Then we can decide what, if anything, is next."

This is just one example. The point is, if you don't take control, your prospect will. As long as you have some rationale about what you're doing, why you're doing it, and that you believe is in everyone's best interest, it will work. I want to leave every meeting with as much information as possible shared in a meaningful way that builds goodwill and differentiates me from everyone else they might be talking to.

There is no way to have a chance of moving through your prospect's concerns and questions if we don't know what they are — ALL of them. When we facilitate a process to have them tell us what they like, what's relevant, etc., we also reinforce our value and relevance in their words, which is much more powerful than using our own descriptions.

Key Reminders:

- The more authentically curious you are, the more information you will get, the more problems you will have a chance to solve, and the more new business you will close.

- Controlling your adrenaline and staying detached from the outcome of your conversation will ensure you get the truth and maintain control.

- A framework of "What I know" and "What I don't know" will help set up your key questions and also put your prospect at ease. Get comfortable with communicating *What you don't know* from a position of strength.

- Find a way to incorporate a Plus/Delta review at the end of all important conversations and negotiations.

YOUR PROCESS FOR ENGAGING PROSPECTIVE CLIENTS

Preview Points:

- Have a process for engaging prospects designed to find out if you are a good fit sooner.
- Be willing to *push back* respectfully on prospects and not just do everything they say.
- Orient your prospect to your process and what to expect next, every step of the way.

Most professionals who are responsible for developing new business haven't given their new client engagement process much thought. Many get caught blindly following their prospect's process and rules of engagement without any questioning, push back, or attempt to take some control. If you have experienced a prospect's process for making buying decisions that is haphazard and inefficient – *where key questions go unanswered, high stakes decision-making gets boiled down to a spreadsheet, and where the main people this big decision impacts are not actively involved* – you have an obligation to lay out other, better options. The prospect can decide to follow you, or not. You can decide if you want to compromise and follow them, or not. In the end, you each have a choice. Is the engagement process a struggle with each party posturing, holding back, and looking for the edge so they don't get taken advantage of? Or is each party open minded, trusting, and coming from a

> *"Having a fundamental structure in your approach actually creates room for creativity and flexibility."*

place of high intent? The stronger and clearer you are about your new prospective client engagement process, the better chance you are going to have to keep control, be efficient, get the truth, and come to a mutually beneficial conclusion in a shorter period of time.

Most of the clients I work with initially struggle with the concept of having a process of their own and the thought of *pushing back* with their prospects. They are so used to going with the flow of what the client wants and bending over backwards in the name of customer service and showing responsiveness, that they have lost sight of some fundamental business sense. I think being responsive, thoughtful, and flexible is great when working with clients on important projects. I find that compulsive, poorly thought out levels of responsiveness can cost organizations large amounts of time and money. And, sadly, this is the norm rather than the exception. One of my clients put it beautifully when she said,

"In an effort to provide superior customer service, we used to react to the urgency voiced on behalf of clients without really understanding even if there was something meaningful to react to. In retrospect, we found in most cases the person in a rush hadn't thought through what they needed, or even worse, they were a liaison to a decision maker who could not make the time to talk to us. This resulted in us producing excellent (expensive) proposals that were doomed.
When everything is hurry up — we now take a deep breath, pause, ask honest questions, and THEN think through what are the best next steps as opposed to being a "dancing monkey." This has resulted in fewer excellent proposals that go nowhere and more proposals that are real and have a potential to make a difference. The result is better use of resources, lower blood pressure, better decision making, and more respect from clients and for ourselves."

—Barbara Allan, Business Owner

Orient the Prospect to Your Process Every Step of the Way

When your prospect is considering change, they are most likely dealing with forces that will resist such changes. It could be the fear in their mind around making a mistake or a boss that has a different perspective than they do. No matter what it is, change is hard for people and there are always forces of resistance at play. Your process needs to be designed with this in mind. The more structure you give your prospect the better. They also need continual reinforcement as to why they are talking to you and considering a change. Your process provides this at each step. The fundamental guiding principles that frame your process are:

> *"They key to closing more deals is to spend more energy looking at process rather than outcomes."*

- Have a process for engaging new prospects.
- Orient prospects and clients to the process and the intent behind each step.
- Stick to it. Don't skip key steps.

People like to know what's coming next and where they stand. Reviewing where we are in the sales process at each step keeps everyone clear. Letting them know what to expect next keeps them calm. If you don't follow steps 1, 2, and 3 above, you will eventually default to the client's process. This is usually not the best way for them to get their problem solved or for finding out if you are in fact the best fit to help them (or not). This is not to say you can't negotiate some elements of your process to make sure your client or prospect gets their needs met. It is important, though, not to automatically default to and follow their process — the trap that most fall into.

In a moment, we will look at a few examples of a client engagement process. There are the steps to the process and the over-arching principles that guide the process. The process lists are effective reminders that there are certain things that need to happen (i.e. information you need, people that must be involved, etc.) at each step in order to move on to the next step. I find that the client engagement process is different for every organization. Use these examples to give you ideas as you think about your process for engaging with new prospective clients and for getting new work from existing clients. The main questions for you are:

Questions to Determine Your Process

- Do you have a process?
- Where does your process most often break down, at what point do you lose control. Why?
- What do you think you or your team need to do more effectively in order to develop and, most importantly, execute a more effective new client engagement process?

As a business professional responsible for generating more work, you have opportunities to talk with clients and new prospects every day, working to identify and solve problems. At least every week, if not every day, you have chances to dig deep and understand what's not working for your prospects and clients. You are constantly running into opportunities to facilitate a process where everyone is transparent and honest and the end result is truly a win-win, even if you don't get the new business. That's a hard one for most of us to swallow – "even if you don't get the new business." I believe it is your responsibility to facilitate a process to give the prospect or client the best possible chance of getting their true problem solved. You walk them through a process that allows them to make a decision that is in their best interest for long-term, sustainable change and significant measurable results. If someone else can help your prospect or client better than you can, then they should get the business. It is your job to be clear about who is and is not a fit for you and your organization and to be perfectly ok with the reality that not everyone is a fit.

Sometimes it's a matter of being clear about your process in typical, seemingly mundane situations. You might have an automatic *default* answer to these questions. What I'd ask is that you consider the way you handle this now might not always be most effective in helping you win more new business and waste less time. Currently...

- When do you send information?
  (at the prospect's request)?
- What do you send?
- When do you drop off information?
- When do you fly to meet someone for
  a meeting or presentation?

I have worked with countless organizations that get caught in this last trap. The moment a prospect shows the smallest amount of interest in talking, they are on the next plane out of town. They are so happy to have to get in front of the prospect, to show their boss they are doing something, and to stay busy that they don't even consider their other options. I'm not suggesting going to visit a prospect in person isn't a good thing. It is often very productive and the right thing to do to close more business. However, we often don't think about what we can accomplish via phone first and how it might be best to prequalify the opportunity before investing time and money into

> *"Most in business to business sales and professional services struggle with HAVING an effective process to take new prospects through, and being DISCIPLINED enough to follow it every time."*

the pursuit. Often in a prospect's process for reviewing new possible vendor-partners they will request (or demand) you fly out for a face-to-face meeting. However, in many instances we move to that step too quickly, before more preliminary communication such as using the phone and email to sufficiently qualify the client. You can go see them, but make sure you have worked your process to a certain extent before hopping on a plane.

One of my business partners was telling me about this experience with their client recently.

"I find they are not coming from a position of strength, but are putting themselves in a one-down position. There was a fair amount of pleading going on – "I would love the opportunity to meet with you", "We would greatly appreciate being considered for your upcoming projects." "You'll talk to me, I'm on the next flight." My client, the top producing account executive, had a breakthrough last week during our call and he said that he was going to have an initial conversation with a perspective client over the phone instead of flying out to see him. When I first met him, he was always going to see people at the drop of a dime and he couldn't seem to understand why that wasn't always the best next step. He's realizing and valuing his time more and he is using it most effectively. This came from me continuing to challenge him on his intent behind everything he's doing and him better understanding his value and the value of his time, and energy."

Below are a few examples of a business-to-business organization's processes for engaging new prospects. As always, your approach should vary based on your particular needs and circumstance. I am not interested in you following a cookie-cutter approach. I want you to develop you own process for engaging new clients and for bidding on new projects from existing clients. If you have your own process, I want you tighten it and, most importantly, implement it more effectively and consistently. Consider using this book to integrate some key guiding principles and a framework that will help ensure your process is effective and not just words on a page. Create clearer guidelines and more structure to give you the best chance to close more of the right kinds of new business faster.

Effective New Client Engagement Process Outline Sample - 1

1. Prospect screening:

- Identify potential prospects based on four main criteria:
- Potential to use our products / services (in general)
- Potential business volume
- Whether or not it is beneficial to take them through the process
- Ensure have all contact info (phone number, email address)

2. Initial cold email/contact

- If no response, send a final interest email
- If response after final interest email, follow step #3

3. If the prospect indicates interest, set up the first conversation

4. Obtain needed information in the first conversation or any follow up conversations.

- Outlined in "Key Questions to Ask" worksheet

5. Determine whether there is a potential fit and/or whether a second conversation is needed

- Possibly with other decision makers in the prospect company

---

- Examine potential red flags (i.e.: if decision makers are involved, if you have satisfactory/honest feedback on the above questions, to name just a few)
- If not a fit, end it

6. **After establishing the initial understanding/relationship we may then discuss the project**
   - It is important to clarify their intent of considering us (what values we are bringing to them), and how they make a choice between us and their other partners. Ideally we request and get feedback after the proposal.

7. **If we have the project, once it is complete, we do project review meeting with the client to discuss what has gone well and what needs to be improved.**

8. **Re-evaluate client relationship annually (or as needed), and see if we may upsell or decide the client may not be as profitable and find ways to improve on that.**

Effective New Client Engagement Process Outline Sample – 2
When you get inbound sales inquiries, here are some questions to help decide if it makes sense to move forward or not:

- How did they hear about us?
- Why are they considering a change from their current supplier?
- Why have they decided to talk with us?
- What other firms are they talking with?
- What is their criteria in choosing a supplier/partner?
- What type of size and volume are their typical projects?
- What is the timing and urgency of this specific project?
- What is their budget for this project?

Effective New Client Engagement Process Sample - 3
Process:
Schedule information conversation
   · Aim for 15-minutes
Ask questions

   · Confirm Decision Maker

   · Company Background/History

   · Current/Future needs

   · Current outsourcing vendors
Identify prospects pain/need
Determine whether the prospect needs our service
   · Can we help with their pain?
Determine if there is a fit

   · Interest in long-term partnership

   · Substantial sales volume

   · Wants vendor involved in research process

   · Willing to put time into relationship

   · Not just looking for price

   · Open to feedback and input from vendor

   · Looking for sole/single vendor

   · Acknowledges value in our company – product / service
   / approach
Does prospect think there is a fit?
Schedule the next call/steps
Identify purpose of next call / next steps
   · Information, negotiating, etc.
Schedule call(s) / meeting(s) until both sides have defined
relationship and both sides feel comfortable

Explain process for submitting RFP/Bids

- Client submit RFP/bid, schedule call to review project specs
- Identify timeline, decision making process etc. on both sides
- Determine if we should bid on project
- Get feedback/pricing/buy-in from department manager
- Complete bid/RFP, schedule follow up conversation once bid sent
- Review project bid — answer questions
- Turn project over to department upon reward

Watch out for the Red Flags

When you are identifying the *red flags* that are most relevant to your business, here are some other things to look for and think about.

- When you get too excited.
- Things are moving too fast (even if they are going well).
- Quick to give a price before you have enough information.
- Prospect is in complete control and not flexible with what they tell you, what they expect, etc.
- You are not sure you're talking to the right person, or all the people who are making this decision.
- You are feeling a lot more attached to getting this deal than they seem committed to solving their problem / doing something different with someone like you.
- You are quoting and presenting solutions before you've asked all of your key questions.

Process for handling Requests for Proposals

Most businesses I work with receive requests for proposals of some kind on a regular basis. This could be a request to submit a "bid" on a particular $10,000 project, a request to present for a $2 million a year consulting contract, or an opportunity to compete with five other money management firms to manage $20 million in assets. Regardless of the size or kind of opportunity, having a process for these situations is the only way to ensure you're not wasting your time working on the wrong opportunities in the wrong ways. Most people that I talk to who are responsible for growing their business automatically assume they are going to answer almost any RFP that comes in the door. Here are a few useful and also "leading" questions to provoke thought and further discussion.

When you receive an RFP...

- Are there questions that you automatically ask yourself?

- Are there typically key *lingering* or unanswered questions that you go back to the client with before completing the task requested?

- Are there ever things that you want to ask or discuss that you don't (because you might think it would be rude or too divergent from their process)?

- Do you have spoken or unspoken guiding principles (process/action or thinking) about answering RFP's?

- Are there any fundamental assumptions you make about this process?

- At what stage do you talk about price and numbers? If you are going to be high do you tell them that up front or is that a discussion for later?

- Do you ever turn down a request for information or proposal? (Initially / After some discussion / Never)

- Are there ways in which you are trying to stand out from others to keep from being commoditized and beat down on price, etc.? Anything you do differently from your competitors?
- Are there key Red Flags that you are looking out for and aware of from the beginning of an RFP process?
- How do you measure success / effectiveness? Are there things you are or are not measuring that are most helpful? Do you know what your conversion rate is? Does this matter?
- What do you think you do really well in this process?
- Are there ways in which you believe you could become more effective and efficient with your RFP response process (preparation / delivery / results)?

In *Moneyball*, Michael Lewis examines how the Oakland Athletics' unique system for finding baseball talent allows them to compete with franchises that spend three-to-four times as much on player payroll. I highly recommend this book for inspiring new ways of looking at and thinking about your business. It is another reminder about the importance of having a process, a system, and a framework of guiding principles that you operate within. Here's an example quoted directly from the book.

"Five simple rules:

1. *No matter how successful you are, change is always good. There can never be a status quo. When you have no money you can't afford long term solutions, only short-term ones. You have to always be upgrading. Otherwise you're f---ed.*

2. *The day you say you HAVE to do something, you're screwed. Because you're going to make a bad deal. You can always recover from the player you didn't sign. You may not recover from the player you signed at the wrong price.*

3. *Know exactly what every player in baseball is worth to you. You can put a dollar figure on it.*

4. *Know exactly who you want and go after him.*

5. *Every deal you do will be publicly scrutinized by subjective opinion."*

Here is another example from a company that I have worked with. These are key reminders they have taped to their desk and reference every time they are talking with a new prospect. These are the things they are most likely to forget about, not look for, or get uncomfortable asking about. Much of this we talked about in the key questions section prior. I think it's worth repeating here as well.

Our sales process key reminders: What we need to know to determine if there is a next step in our conversation with a prospect (Not in any particular order):

- *Who else cares about this?*

- *Why do you decide to change (talking to me/looking for new options/ pains/problems?) Why not keep doing what you have been doing?*

- *Business volume (overall revenue/size, potential business for us).*

- *Urgency/timing.*

- *Decision-making process/important factors in working with a partner/ how do they use information we provide if they request additional information?*

- *What's it worth to them/cost of not solving the problem/benefit of solving the problem.*

- *Are they open to our engagement process? (Note, beware sometimes prospects just say they are open so they can get information/costs from us.)*

- *Pricing/budget/expectations.*

My experience has been that 99% of the time, business leaders and sales professionals send information and travel to meetings too early in the process. Before they have done a good job of qualifying the opportunity, they are quickly firing off a ton of information or jumping on an airplane to "get in front of" the prospect. Before sending info or catching a flight, have a conversation or two first. Value your time as much as you do your prospect's.

The System is the Star

The organizations with the best patterns of growth have created a system and a culture that are bigger than any one person. With the exception of the owner, president, or key leader, no one else is more important than the system. The system is the organization's unique philosophy for doing business, how it approaches new opportunities, and its process of attracting or scaring off new clients that allows it to be in control. The right system is even more important than having a bunch of all-star talent.

Talent is important, of course. And, as you know full well, high-priced talent often comes with big egos and a lack of openness to new ways of doing business. I believe there needs to be a balance of an effective system and the right people that fit that system. If you lead an organization or have the ability to influence the company at systemic levels, this is your challenge: to create a new system that all the players buy into.

As you build this system, implement it well, and start to see results, it will also impact the organizational culture and morale. If you are interested in this and up for the challenge of a year long (or more) process to implement it and have it stick, you will be in for a pleasant surprise. At the risk of being dramatic, the implementation of the guiding principles and approaches to your thinking, language, and process for growing your business will change you personally. They will change the way you look at yourself and the way others perceive you. They will change the results you get and how you feel in the process of getting them.

Another example of the system and its underlying principles from outside of traditional business is again from Moneyball by Michael Lewis. Even without the context of reading the book, this gives you some other ways to look at setting up your system and the importance of thinking differently and having others within the organization buy in.

> *"Once he decided that hitting was the most important tool and everything else was secondary, Alderson set about implementing throughout the organization, with Marine Corps rigor, a uniform approach to hitting. The approach had three rules:*
>
> > *1. Every batter needs to behave like a leadoff man,*
> > *and adopt as his main goal getting on base.*
>
> > *2. Every batter should also possess the power to hit home runs,*
> > *in part because home run power forced opposing pitchers to pitch more*
> > *cautiously, and led to walks, and high-on-base percentages.*
>
> > *3. To anyone with the natural gifts to become a professional baseball player,*
> > *hitting was less a physical than a mental skill. Or, at any rate,*
> > *the aspects of hitting that could be taught were mental.*
>
> *By 1995 Alderson had created a new baseball corporate culture around a single baseball statistic: on-base percentage. Scoring runs was, in the new view, less an art or a talent than a process. If you made the process a routine – if you got every player doing his part on the production line – you could pay a lot less for runs than the going rate. Alderson was building a system with Marine Corps intolerance for exceptions to the rules.*
>
> *...The system's central tenet was, in Alderson's words, "the system was the star. The reason the system works is that everyone buys into it. If they don't,*

there is a weakness in the system." The unacceptable vice in a minor league player was a taste for bad pitches. The most praiseworthy virtue was the willingness to take a base on balls."

— Michael Lewis, Moneyball

As a professional, I imagine that you put forth a lot of energy, study, and attentiveness to your craft, your business, and your proprietary knowledge. Whether you are the president of a high tech consulting company, a high end money manager, corporate CPA, or field sales rep, you spend time and effort focusing on knowing and learning more about your business, your products, and your services. You are an expert at what you do, right?

Not too long ago I was talking with a prospective client in the financial services and consulting business for high net worth individuals and organizations. He perfectly summed up the need for more focus on a business development-related process, a system, and skill-building in new areas. After discussion and reflection, he said he realized his company and it's leadership needed to "Bring the same discipline to sales and marketing that we do to investment management." I believe a more disciplined and focused approach to your efforts for engaging new prospects and deepening relationships with current clients is the only way to sustainably grow, without great struggle. It's also a much better way to live.

Key Reminders:

- Develop and follow your process and guiding principles to ensure you are on track, notify you when you've veered off course, and warn you when you are best served to walk away.

- The questions you ask your clients, the way you walk them through the process, what you uncover, and your intent, all give you a unique opportunity to set yourself apart from the competition.

- Create a system / approach / process that is bigger than any one person and build it into your culture. Make this a part of how you and your team think, act, and talk every day with clients. Your process and how you engage with clients create points of differentiation between you and your competition beyond differences in service or product. Dare to be different, thoughtful, bold, and savvy in the process you take new prospects and existing clients through to get new business.

STRUCTURE & SPONTANEITY

Preview Points:

- Having more structure to your new client engagement process actually frees you up to be more spontaneous and present.

- Your intuition about what question to ask and what next step to take is most likely right on target. Know when and how to trust it.

- The better you can get at "managing the moment" with prospects, the more people you will help and money you will make.

Structure & Spontaneity: Optimal skill & discipline for managing the moment.

Now that you have a number of new elements of process structure, guiding principles, and even specific language scripts, let's talk about spontaneity. This entire approach is about heightened levels of disciplined awareness, effective preparation, and consistent structure. At the same time, what I am suggesting is also an approach that is about having the freedom to be spontaneous and fully in the moment during your conversations with prospects and in any high stakes negotiations. I realize this may seem paradoxical, but they actually fit together perfectly. It's only by having a structured approach and superior preparation - of your thinking, your language, and your process - that you can be freed up to better listen and respond to your clients. This structure, or framework, supports you in listening more effectively, asking better questions, and providing answers that are specifically relevant to their needs.

The misperception that people have in initial conversations with me about the work I do and how it might be relevant for them or their organization is that it's all about process and structure. They are either excited or spooked by the idea of having a disciplined, rigid, point-by-point, structured process they take clients through. Much of this book has been dedicated to laying out more structured approaches to the client engagement process and ways that you can gain and maintain more control of that process. Truth is, that's only half the story.

This approach will not work optimally if you are just rigidly checking off boxes and robotically reading scripts. I do want you to have a strong framework, key steps, and guiding principles. But I also want you to be human and flexible when appropriate. This is a learned skill, although some natural talent will certainly help. "The key process elements" and "The scripted language" are only optimally effective if you are able to inject yourself and your personality into them. Getting people that don't know you to open up to talking with you, meeting with you, and sharing important information with you is all about trust.

Our discussion until now has prepared you to be able to anticipate questions before they are asked. Simply following your process and using your scripted words mechanically can create blind spots. This often keeps you from making adjustments in the moment and capitalizing on opportunities that arise unexpectedly. For optimal effectiveness at developing more of the right kinds of new business there has to be room for spontaneity. The spontaneity is actually created by the presence of the structure / framework that holds everything together.

Having access to and being able to trust your intuition is an essential aspect to an optimally successful new business development presentation or negotiation. The key is being able to "slow things down" when it seems like everything is happening quickly and you feel put on the spot. Professional athletes, musicians, and other people at the top of their game talk about being "in the zone." It's the same thing in high stakes sales calls, business negotiation, and presentations. To succeed, you need to be able to drop down into the zone, where you are at a different level of awareness. From this place there is less emotion and fewer distractions from hyperactive thoughts. You are focused, present, and your heart rate is normal.

Getting to this place is not quite as simple as describing it. The first step is realizing when you're NOT in it. Catch yourself when you are breathing more heavily or your breath is more shallow than normal. Notice when you feel like you're talking too much, when you're face gets flush, or your body feels like its getting overheated. I'll say it again: slow down. Take a breath. Shut up for a second. Relax. Remind yourself to follow your process. No one is going to die if you don't get the business. You might have a heart attack if you don't relax a bit, though. Find your own routine for preparing for a "big" meeting and for catching yourself when you get off track and bringing yourself back. If you have particular physical or mental techniques for accomplishing this, please share them at www.perficency.com/presence.

> *"In the moment of truth, the great athletes lose total self awareness and even lack of consciousness of what's going on. He becomes egoless."*
> — Bruce Ogilvie

The structure that I have suggested up to this point actually leads to more freedom. It frees you up to be more present, more spontaneous, more human, and more yourself. In order to execute at high level in sales and negotiation, and still come across naturally, it takes a lot of awareness, discipline, and preparation. I have not found a better analogy for this than Malcolm Gladwell's description of an improv comedy group. I might be the first person to compare selling to improvisational comedy, but bear with me for a moment.

"Improvisation comedy is a wonderful example of the kind of thinking that Blink is all about. It involves people making very sophisticated decisions on the spur of the moment, without the benefit of any kind of script or plot. That's what makes it so compelling and — to be frank — terrifying... Every word and movement has been scripted. Every performer gets to rehearse. There's a director in charge, telling everyone what to do. Now suppose that I were to ask you to perform again before a live audience — only this time without a script, without any clue as to what part you were playing or what you were supposed to say, and with the added requirement that you were expected to be funny. I'm quite sure you'd rather walk on hot coals. What is terrifying about improv is the fact that it appears utterly random and chaotic. It seems as though you have to get up on stage and make everything up, right there on the spot. But the truth is that improv isn't random and chaotic at all. If you were to sit down with the case of (this improv group), for instance, and talk to them at length, you'd quickly find out that they aren't all the sort of zany, impulsive, free-spirited comedians that you might imagine them to be. Some are quite serious, even nerdy. Every week they get together for a lengthy rehearsal. After each show they gather backstage and critique each other's performance soberly. Why do they practice so much? Because improv is an art form governed by a series of rules, and they want to make sure that when they're up on stage, everyone abides by those rules. "We think of what we're doing as a lot like basketball."... Basketball is an intricate, high speed game filled with split second, spontaneous decisions. But that spontaneity is possible only when everyone first engages in hours of highly repetitive and structured practice — perfecting shooting, dribbling, passing and running plays over and over again — and agrees to play a carefully defined role on

the court. This is the critical lesson of improv, too…: spontaneity isn't random….How good people's decisions are under the fast-moving, high stress conditions of rapid cognition is a function of training and rules and rehearsal."

—Malcolm Gladwell, Blink

In order for people to get a sense of whether or not they want to do business with you, they must get a sense that you understand them, can help them, and have something unique (about you and/or your organization) to offer. In order to effectively uncover and convey these things you must be *present*. By present I mean fully in the moment, not thinking about other things or worrying about your next "move." The more able you are to be present with your prospect, the more business you will win. In order to do this with optimal effectiveness you cannot move too fast or too slow. Your job is to hear what your prospect is saying and at the same time keep the process moving forward. Help them clarify and understand what they want and need, why that's important, and who is going to be the best fit to help them.

Running stairs is a part of my exercise routine. While working my way up the stairs, recently, it struck me as a perfect metaphor for what I teach related to the new business development process. Both are about staying fully focused on what's right in front of you, one step at a time. But if you can, preparing for the steps in advance can improve your final result. Have an idea of what your plan is before heading up the incline. When you're climbing, one step at a time, it's much safer to ALSO have an idea of what's coming next.

Your primary focus should be on what's right in front of you, with clear, hard eyes, while also having a sense of what's coming next as your secondary state of focus, with open, soft eyes. When I'm teaching people to facilitate a new business conversation, I want the person to have a sense of what's going to happen for the whole conversation, focus specifically on the present moment, and have an idea at each transition point what needs to happen next. I want them to be aware of where things are going and be able to share that vision with others. I want them to be clear, confident, and taking the lead, while also appearing flexible and engaging to their prospect. Engaging them in a way where they feel a sense of buy-in to process. This is a delicate dance.

As a professional responsible for developing new business, your job is to effectively "*manage the moment.*" In this state you are fully present in the moment and at the same time always one half-step ahead.

> "*Extraordinary performances come out of a process of continuous, regular physical and mental practice. The mindset of an extraordinary athlete is relaxed but focused and open to even higher achievements.*"
> — Jerry Laughlin

Key Reminders:

- Every bit of preparation and structure to your new client engagement process allows for equal amounts of spontaneity in the moment.

- You are not a robot. Interject yourself, your personality, and your style into the process and language elements of this approach.

- Stay present in the moment, asking and listening intently while simultaneously having a sense of what's coming next at all times. People are looking to be led.

EMOTIONS AND THE REACTIVE MIND

Preview Points:

- The more aware you are of your thought process and how it affects your actions, the more control you will have in all situations.

- We are mostly reacting to circumstances and are not in control of our thoughts, emotions, and actions — especially in high stakes negotiation, difficult communication, and emotionally charged situations.

- The mind never turns off — it is always working to protect you, keep you safe, minimize your pain, and maximize your pleasure.

- Much of the mindset / thinking that got you to this point is actually holding you back from getting to the next level in your career mastery and life success.

"We see a tiny fragment of reality — one that allows us to master our physical environment — and little more."
—Jeff Salz, The Way of Adventure

The More Aware You Are of the Content of Your Thinking and How It Affects Your Actions, the More Control You Will Have in All Situations.

Many of the highly successful business professionals I know are amateur psychologists. They have a clear handle on their own thinking, reactions, and emotions. They also understand the behaviors and cues of the person sitting across the table. They are driven to win more new business, but never show they care more about getting a deal done than their prospective new client. In sales situations, they have a passion for solving problems, love a challenge, and at the same time display a sense of calm detachment from the specific outcome they are negotiating.

How often have you been in a situation where someone thought you and your product/service were great? They openly shared their need for your service and energetically told you so much that you thought you had a "done deal." Then, when it came time for the next step in the process, they flaked out on you and disappeared. How often have you had a formal presentation or conversation with a prospect where you believed it to be crystal clear that your solution was clearly the best choice to solve their problem? You knew you could help them but they just didn't see it. We, as humans, on the buying or selling side of things, are operating on *automatic pilot* much of the time. We often don't know why we don't do what we know we should do. Something holds us back (i.e.: fear of making a mistake, fear of change, avoidance of the conflict, etc.).

Influenced by our genetics, childhood upbringing, and circles of influence, we all end up "hard-wired" in a way that controls our life. Much of our identification with our ego comes from early childhood experiences. I am not going to analyze your "strained" connection to your dad or "over-dependent" relationship with your mother. I do want to point out that many of these habitual patterns of thinking and reacting come from deep within you. It is important and helpful to understand, at least at some basic level, how you're wired. Because this wiring gets laid down and reinforced over-and-over for years, starting at birth, it becomes naturally and effortlessly habitual, reactive, and unconscious. These wired patterns can work against your efforts to get new results. You can't change unless you're creating pattern interrupts and carving new neuropathways in your brain. Repeated exposure to new experiences and different ways of doing the same thing will slowly re-program our old, *default* ways of thinking and being.

> *"There are dozens, maybe hundreds of unconscious, unexamined beliefs that run your life from the subterranean levels of shadowy awareness — beliefs about your worthiness and competence, for example, or whether people can be trusted or not — that were deposited in childhood and continue to determine how you relate to the world."*
> — William Arntz, Betsy Chasse, Mark Vicente,
> What the Bleep Do We Know!?

The Limbic Brain consists of the Amygdala, located at the base of the brain stem, and houses the structure for our emotional memory. Our emotions literally have a mind of their own, a view quite independent of our rational brain. This emotional memory is constantly scanning, comparing present situations to past situations and emotional reactions. It is looking for a "match" or recognizable pattern. This process is designed to put things in categories of understanding, make sense of the world, and in particular keep you safe from being hurt or surprised. Your emotional memory helps you survive by giving you a lightening-quick reference that puts the puzzle together before you even understand the pieces.

The problem with this system is that it's a raw, unsophisticated, and often a sloppy circuit. It triggers a reaction immediately, before getting complete confirmation of a match between current and past experience. This raw emotion gets triggered independent of and prior to any rational thought. Even as the neocortex — the problem solving, rational part of the brain - is processing and making a decision, the emotional part of our brain has often already taken over. When this takes

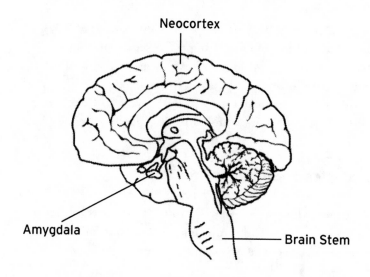

over, you become reactive, compulsively trying to protect your-self from "harm." The brain loses blood, which moves to the body preparing to literally, physically flee the scene. This is a very old, unsophisticated response wired into us for hundreds (maybe thousands) of years. When this happens, our ability to hear others is significantly impaired, if not shut off entirely. Our blood is pumping, our heart is racing, and any unrelated or unnecessary movements are frozen.

This system has served us quite well in our evolutionary past. If you were a caveman, it would happen the moment you spotted a Saber Tooth tiger staring you down from 20 feet away. The problem is that it's crude and the predators and situa-tions it was designed to keep us safe from don't exist anymore. And often, the things we're having reactions to are not actually real at all. It's our perception of a situation, an over reaction caused by past experiences in relation to a current situation. So we overreact or shut down in situations where staying open and engaged is what is most called for. This can happen to you in a tough presentation, high-stakes negotiation, or uncomfortable conversation. It can also happen to your prospects. We are all vulnerable to getting triggered, especially when the stakes are high, emotions are running hot, and attachment and fear are hiding just beneath the surface. These imprinted emotional memories run deep and long, and can be faulty guides to the reactions and thinking needed in the present moment.

Examples of Stored Event "Tags":

Event - The president walks into the room as you're speaking and you quickly lose your place, blank out, and start stammering. You feel embarrassed and stupid.

Event - Your boss calls you out in a meeting showing his displeasure with the new business update you gave him. Your mind starts racing with thoughts about losing your job, how long will your savings last, when Joey's college tuition payment due, that your wife is going to be pissed, etc. You are momentarily terrified and then angry.

"We walk through the door into the organization every morning looking like full-grown adults, but many parts of us are still playing emotional catch up. The griefs and traumas of childhood follow us around, asking for attention."
—David Whyte, The Heart Aroused

The longer you live and the more experiences you have, the more memories you have stored in your brain. When something new happens that matches a stored experience you get triggered like it was the first time, although with more emotional energy that comes from having experienced this multiple times. We have a strong desire NOT to feel that feeling and have that experience again.

The brain has a multitude of connections that allow it to find the most important memories first. This helps make sure that you don't forget something really important like how putting your hand on the stove will burn and cause significant pain. Or how holding an open cup of hot coffee while your teenager drives may cause a mess, make you angry, and possibly burn your lower extremities. You remember the time you fell through the ice at the lake and therefore are hyper-aware of the conditions needed for safe ice-skating. Instead of being able to evaluate a new experience from a fresh perspective, we almost always assume — at an unconscious level — that it is an experience we've already had. Therefore, our responses to that stimulus keep repeating themselves. The mechanism that is designed as a shortcut to help us survive actually traps us into doing the same thing over and over.

Bottom Line: We Are Emotional Creatures First

We are triggered by past events that may not having anything to do with the present. We create "tags" in our brain to help us sort out the good from the bad. As a professional responsible for developing new business, your awareness of these tags for yourself and your prospect will help you more effectively manage the process of new client engagement and negotiation.

Mental Chatter

One of the biggest obstacles we have in our desire for more success, personal achievement, life balance, and happiness is the constant chatter in our heads. Our mind literally never shuts off. It's constantly active with thoughts and processing information. We spend most of our time swimming in thoughts, ideas, fears, and excitements that don't move us closer to getting more of what we want (i.e.: better clients, more money, more meaningful relationships). Notice this mental chatter - the voices in your head and the things you're juggling that are taking most of your energy and focus. Notice when you are not present in this moment, with the person in front of you, but are instead thinking of something else and did not hear a word they just said. The better job you do quieting the chatter, the more present you will be and the better you will be at picking up on the clues and messages your prospect is giving you, and information that will both help you better be able to help them and win you more business.

> *"Ninety percent of the mind's running commentary on our lives is not in the least relevant to our circumstances."*
> —Maria Nemeth, The Energy of Money

Our compulsively working brain is the cause of most of our pain. There is pain related to outside circumstances and life events. Ninety-five percent of the time, we are thinking about, worried about, or reacting to things that haven't happened, aren't happening, or won't happen. As our brain works to keep us safe and happy, in many ways it's sabotaging our ability to enjoy the moment, not overreact, and create an optimal environment for success. We get caught in a web that repeats itself. Getting unstuck is very possible, although not easy.

> *"The human brain is the only object in the known universe that can predict its own future and tell it own fortune. The fact that we can make disastrous decisions even as we foresee their consequences is the great, unsolved mystery of human behavior."*
> — Daniel Gilbert, Stumbling on happiness

We get addicted to these states and can't get ourselves out. It sounds crazy. After all, why would you want to remain in my current situation and not have more success, happiness, and fulfillment? Well, a part of your brain does not want to change. What you're doing right now is feeding it. Your status quo is keeping it / you feeling safe and secure. It will fight you tooth and nail if you try and change. It will distract you and try to get you to give up your quest for change. There is a part of your brain, that even though uncomfortable, even unhappy, does not want to change. It is comfortable with the current pattern of thoughts and habitual actions. Although you thought it was just for "crazy people" you do have a voice (or two) inside your head. The more aware you are of this and the better you understand it, the less likely it will be to control you.

The brain is actually well-meaning. It does believe it is doing you a service and is helping you. But many times, the old programming it is projecting onto your current reality is completely irrelevant. Charged, stressful, high stakes, or difficult sales, negotiation, and communication situations are an ideal place to practice facing these old thoughts and emotional tags and rewiring them.

> *"The best way that a human being can become that observer is, first of all, having the awareness or the understanding intellectually that they don't always have to make the same choices over and over again. And second, be put in certain situations, experimentally, in your own personal (and professional life) where you actually override those mechanisms in your body and that takes practice."*
> —Joe Dispenza, What the Bleep Do We Know!?

I have a client who, when we first met, had a strong tendency to want to please everyone. This is simultaneously a strength (he takes great care of all of his clients) and a weakness (he gets overwhelmed by all the demands from all of his clients, many of whom were difficult and unprofitable). During a group training session with his team, it became clear that he needed to turn down a new prospect who was begging for his help. In the past he would have never turned anyone away. He felt that if he turned this prospect down, he would be a "bad person," would feel guilty, and, at the risk of being dramatic, - there was something about it that was so painful, it was like he "just might die." In the face of this prospect's sad-sack begging and the wrath of his eventual anger, my client told this prospect that he had to "respectfully decline to help him on this project."

He did not die, but was very uncomfortable. This was the first time he faced his fear - of not being everyone's friend and always accommodating others – head-on. He risked the wrath, judgment, and guilt that can go along with telling someone "no." Turns out, there were no real negative consequences, either to him or the business. It did free him up to spend more time on his better clients. He was on his way to breaking a pattern, re-programming a neuronet in his brain. The next time he said "no," to a prospect it was easier. He is now an old pro at it, but every now and then he'll get squeamish about not responding to an RFP or turning down a prospect that is not a good fit.

Recently, I was working with a client who was desperately afraid to miss out on any opportunity to bid on new projects. So, he created a system where he answered everything that came into his office. He bid on every project with zero regard for the likelihood his organization would actually get the project, if they were really set up to do a good job on the project, or how profitable the project would be. So, he spent twenty plus hours every week frantically sending out all the information that his clients requested. He nearly burnt himself out in the process, afraid that the one thing that he doesn't respond to might be the big deal that he would forever regret passing on.

The most interesting part of this from, my viewpoint, is the compulsiveness that drives the action. There is little or no regard for the strategic thinking about what he is doing and why, and how he might be more optimally effective with his time and energy. He's just doing what he does, and what makes him the most comfortable – or the least uncomfortable might be more accurate. Once I spent some time looking at his process for answering bid requests and helping him better filter the good and bad requests, he began to see things a little differently (albeit slowly). I challenged him to look closely at where he was spending his time and energy. He was already working fifty hours a week. I pointed out if he wanted to get ahead in his organization and increase his end of the year bonus, he was going to have to work smarter, not harder.

After some research and reflection, he realized there was one recurring request he got every week that was taking up approximately 20 hours of his time during the course of the month. From all of those hours, he had produced only $10,000 of business during the year (when his best clients were spending $200,000 per year). Now, I don't know what rate you're used to getting compensated at, or your expectations of a time and money return, but this is a colossal inequity of return on his investment of time and energy. Something had to change.

He talked with the client and figured out a way to spend about an hour a month giving them some (but not all) of what they needed to at least keep him in the running for some of the projects. That was just one situation that carved out 19 hours of time! I don't use exclamation points often, but I think it's appropriate here. I am not suggesting you have such a dramatic example of compulsive behavior that is creating wasted time and effort in your business development process, but everyone's process can use some fine-tuning.

Think of all the fear that comes with sales – fear of losing an opportunity, of not getting the business, and ultimately of looking bad (to our boss, co-workers, spouse, prospects, clients). Most manipulative attempts to control and persuade a new prospect or client are based on fear. We jump at every request a new prospect or client makes. Now, I'm not suggesting you not be accommodating, flexible, or aim to please. I am suggesting that for most business professionals this pendulum has swung way too far to one side where the prospects and clients have all the control. You, the provider of a service to them, are following along without any thought of how both parties can most effectively make a decision about whether or not you should do business together. What is your automatic default mindset in situations where one client makes demands? In the end, if you become more savvy about these things and less afraid, I promise you will actually close MORE business, not less.

Some of you know it to be true. Others might think I'm nuts. Let me remind you again that although some of the things I suggest might seem "soft," "self-defeating," or "just plain nuts," that my goal in all that I do is to help you win more of the right kinds of new business with the least amount of wasted effort. Consider that at times you try too hard, not try hard enough at other times, or can even be lazy regarding certain activities.

Here is a note I received from a client. We were working at getting her more "detached" and to an even level with her clients. Instead of scurrying around and dropping everything to meet a client's complex demands in a request for a proposal, she was more thoughtful about her reactions. It's not that she became disinterested and unhelpful. It's that she found a more appropriate balance, was less likely to feel unnecessary pressure, and more apt to work her process. She trusted that, in the end, the right clients would be willing to be reasonable and thoughtful about their working relationships, communication, and expectations regarding her.

"I got a call on a Wednesday afternoon from a client. He called all excited about an extra $150k he now had to spend. He had lots of big ideas. He said he needed my proposal by Friday, end of day. I told him that I was going to be out on vacation the next 2 days. That I can start the process of getting what he wants and get things going, but we might need a bit more time. He said that was unacceptable and he needed it by end of day Friday.

This was a case where it really wasn't reasonable to get it done in this timeline, and if we did, it would be a huge strain on a number of people. He pushed back. "I would absolutely understand if you need to move forward because we can't get it to you on Friday, and we would not be considered for this particular RFP."

Mindset: I knew I wasn't going to be able to get it done and wasn't going to over commit and over promise. He was calling me last minute and to really give him a good answer, I would need more time. I was totally honest and matter of fact and understood if he needed to do something without us.

He told me that we "Have to be on the plan," and spent the next ten minutes telling me why we have to be a part of this plan and our importance to him. He was saying things like, "Please don't not do it." You have to do it." He was literally selling me. It was almost funny. I wasn't afraid of losing the business. Deep down I knew we could only do so much, realistically. I got him back into MY process, not defaulting automatically to HIS process. I got something to him the following Tuesday and it was all perfectly fine."

Here is another note from a client that also relates to "The Power of Emotional Detachment." We had been working on how he could be even more bold and willing to acknowledge the full reality of things out loud. Meaning, to be ok talking about what he could do and what he couldn't do and why to hire him and why not to hire him. We also worked on facilitating a process where he got the prospect to put everything on the table, to share honestly about what they like, what their concerns are, etc. In order to have a more honest and productive conversation, you have to be willing to hear what you don't want to hear and even risk losing the business.

"Tom, something great happened today. My company is on step eight in negotiations with a billion dollar healthcare organization. It has been the perfect example of the complex sale.

We met with individuals that were clearly not open to us at the beginning. We all went into it not knowing what to expect and really anticipating closure to our potential engagement. The prospects were clearly not in support of what we were offering. Despite the meeting being on the phone, it was clear that their walls were up. What did we do? We did not sell.
We had a conversation with them. We provided a history of our relationship together and what we have been through to get us here. We also stated that everyone has been skeptical of us because of our size and some specifics about our solution. We were under no illusions that they were not skeptical, too.

All of the sudden, everything started to shift. We were matter of fact and very transparent about who we are, why we were there, what we do, and how we see things. We then talked about potential objections that we thought they had but weren't sharing. What ended up happening is that our advocate picked up the ball and started selling us to her colleagues internally. It was amazing. Our champion started doing the selling. She jumped in and said, "They are undervaluing themselves and this is what they are doing and this is why it is important to us." Note to self: When that happens, shut up and let them talk. No selling required. We took a resistant audience and got them on our side.

We went into this meeting thinking this was probably the end of this opportunity. We prepared a lot in advance, as much on our mindset and our language as on anything else. We were all on the same page and were not emotionally attached to the outcome. This allowed us to be fully present, ask good questions, and own up to the objections we have received in advance of them sharing them. This kept us in control without even trying. It was almost funny how, by backing off and not trying to sell and even being willing to talk about the objections they may have about us right up front, all of a sudden the dynamics changed. As you say, we "created space" and then they came toward us. Our advocate stepped up and did the work and her peers followed.

Result: They are helping us get further funding and they want to move forward with the pilot. This is a big victory.

Damn, this is getting easier and easier every time we do it. It should be. If you are emotionally detached, you ask the right questions. If you follow your process, the outcome takes care of itself. Besides, it no longer is called sales. It is called having conversation and evaluating whether there is mutual benefit and the value you bring. These kinds of results don't happen overnight. When they do come, it's the best feeling in the world."

"The paradox of reaching your goals is that you must work actively toward them, and at the same time detach yourself from them. Do the things you know will get you there and obsess less about them on a daily basis."

Notice, understand, and then face your fears. Have honest conversations. Increase your awareness of compulsive behaviors that are driven by fear (of losing the business, of making someone mad, etc.). The more you understand what's going on in your over-active mind (as well as the mind of your prospect), the less time you will waste running around like a chicken with its head cut off. You will get more opportunities to help more people, solve more problems, and make more money.

Key Reminders:
- Remember: We are emotional creatures first. The process of buying and selling is an emotional and human one.
- Bill Caskey, author of *Same Game, New Rules* says, "Never be a hostage to your own emotional needs and desires. Never make your prospect a hostage to those needs either." Keep your emotions and needs to yourself. Don't let your prospect or client see you sweat or appear needy and overly excited.
- You can change your actions, but if you don't also work on changing your thinking, you will not be able to sustain your new results over time.

LEARNING & CHANGE

Preview Points:
- Sustained change requires a disciplined effort over time and must tolerate feelings of discomfort.
- More information and knowledge has little correlation to your ability to change.
- Increased awareness and new daily actions give you the best chance for new results that stick.

"Research in neuroscience and cognitive science shows that people remember and respond most effectively to what they see and experience... On the other hand, experiences that don't involve touching, seeing, or feeling actual results, such as being presented with an abstract sheet of numbers, are shown to be non-impactful and easily forgotten. Tipping point leadership builds upon this insight to inspire a fast change in mindset that is internally drive of people's own accord. Instead of relying on numbers to tip the cognitive hurdle, they make people experience the need for change in two ways."
— W. Chan Kim and Renee Mauborgne, Blue Ocean Strategy

Learning and Change

The drive to build sustainable, growth-oriented organizations is a part of the fabric of our modern business culture. In the U.S. in particular, the battle for highly skilled, sophisticated workforce talent is more heated than ever. The margin for error these days is small. The wrong hire or the lack of development by a key leader or sales professional can have dire consequences for the organization, both short and long term. I have seen entire organizations implode because their leadership did not have the skills and mindset to deal with crises or a much-needed change in thinking and strategy. I've seen a lack of awareness of personal and interpersonal psychology derail leaders and sales professionals. Developing a more sophisticated level of awareness and skills in the areas of personal psychology, interpersonal communication, and business process and strategy is vital for success.

As a business leader, you cannot just look at the surface issues. You must have the courage to look at what's beneath the surface. This is sometimes painful and even potentially embarrassing. Any unwillingness to having these conversations with yourself and your team is holding you back. Be willing to get radically honest with yourself and those around you about what really is working in your efforts to grow your business. Most importantly, be willing to have an honest conversation about what's NOT working, without blame, fear, or judgment (easier said than done). Are you willing to dig into why certain efforts or results are not working, what needs to shift, and how you might be contributing to the problem?

> *"Too often in business we get caught in the trap of equating activity with productivity. The correlations between the two are not nearly as tight as we like to think."*

Make More Calls

What is the underlying cause of the lack of results? Is it that you aren't making enough calls or you're not closing enough of the deals in your pipeline? That is the symptom, but the underlying cause is related to your thinking, your language in your approach, and your process. A thoughtful and comprehensive approach to digging deeper is needed to understand what is not working and to create a plan to fix it. This is not as simple as "make more calls." If that approach works, it will only be for a week, or month, or maybe more, if you're lucky, before things return to their old state. We have to work on the underlying causes, not just the symptoms, to produce real change. And we have to be more sophisticated about our questions and our exploration of what's not working. The filters to run this through that I've found most beneficial are ones you've heard a lot about in this book. Again, the three filters are: **Thinking, Language** and **Process.**

If you want to make quantum leaps and fundamental shifts, you have to look deeper, down into the root causes in a way that explores both the psychology and strategy of business to business sales and personal achievement.

The ego also wants you to be perfect and has little tolerance for mistakes. This is the destructive force to learning and growth. To learn to practice what I am suggesting consistently, you must develop a high tolerance for making mistakes. What happens here is that you become hyper-aware of what is and is not working (your Thinking, Language, and Process). As you realize how many things you're doing are NOT working this can paralyze you, if your ego gets a hold of you. The ego has little capacity for self-compassion and the necessary patience it takes to integrate this new framework of thinking and doing business. It takes most people at least a year to fully implement it, and even then they need reinforcements to ensure it "sticks."

The ego wants quick results. The ego does not want to feel the pain of struggling as your build yourself back up again. The ego will even try to convince you that *"To create an optimal environment or learning, you just remove fear from the environment."* you already know and practice all the things in this book, even when that's not the case. You will be tempted to believe it. This is much easier than doing the hard work necessary to grow to new levels of awareness and discipline in your thinking, your language, and your process for engaging with clients. As much as increasing your level of competence and ability to sell yourself and your company from a position of strength, this approach is also about being human and transparent. I want you to stand out in a truly unique way so your clients realize they can't get YOU anywhere else. When you reach this point, you have no competition.

In order to get to this place, you do have to take more risks, make some mistakes, and be more vulnerable. When I use this word I don't mean it from a place of weakness or meekness or crying or hugging. You can come from a position of authenticity and strength and still be vulnerable. Most of us are deathly afraid of rejection. The more you can almost dare them to reject you and be totally ok with it, the more business you will attract. New prospects will be drawn to you, trust you, and believe you can help them. Strength, wisdom, success, authenticity, and vulnerability don't have to be mutually exclusive.

Shifting Self-perception

Besides the philosophies and approaches in this book, one theme that I have tried to convey is the importance of creating a shift in the perception you have of yourself. Sales and any kind of business development activities provide a unique opportunity to see yourself, face your fears, and try new ways of interacting with the world. The bonus is that as you get better at these things, you make more money and help more people. As you are doing your own self-guided learning, or leading a team through new learning activities, use the filters of single, double, and triple-loop learning. Dig beneath the surface of the symptoms and work on the thinking and fears behind actions. Set up a culture that supports and challenges you and your team to execute new behaviors and get different results. Look deeper than just the surface symptoms and quick fixes. Is your approach really getting to the heart of the matter and does it have a chance to create some level of sustainable change? Or is it just going through the motions, checking off boxes, and having everyone robotically do what they are supposed to do without true engagement or legitimately duplicatable results?

Making the Theoretical Real

One of the simplest yet most transformative elements of optimal learning I've seen is taking classroom learning and applying into real world experience. If there are new ideas and approaches that you've learned, the best way to find out if they work, change your habits, and make them effective is to apply, apply, and apply again to your daily life. Ideally, you will have a coach, mentor, or peer learner with whom you can pre-brief and de-brief about your experiences.

"Difference between belief and KNOWLEDGE — importance of experience (experiential learning — making abstractions/philosophy REAL), which leads to wisdom. I have knowledge when I have experienced that thing personally, and if I, for instance, walked on water, I would have knowledge that it is possible to do, and I could never again doubt it really. But if I only believe it on the word of somebody else, well, then it's only a philosophy, an abstraction, and a great necessity in evolution is to change belief into knowledge or into experience or into wisdom. To convert knowledge into wisdom that is experienced is that great journey of our spiritual development."
—William Arntz, Betsy Chasse, Mark Vicente,
What the BLEEP Do We Know!?

Get Off the Bandwagon—Stop Searching for the Next "Big Thing"

One of the points I touched upon in the early parts of the book is how we look outside of ourselves for answers. Now, I believe strongly that it is a good idea to get outside support when you need it. But, there are so many organizational leaders who are just looking for the next magical answer to their problems. Every few years there is a new fad to create a more effective organization, be more successful, be more productive, etc. Within all of these fads there are some good ideas. More often than not, though, they don't get executed well in the field and are not sustainable. This happens so often that I see most business professionals have become jaded against any NEW idea. They are skeptical that this is just going to be just the same thing—get excited, start something, and then go back to our old ways.

There is no quick fix and everyone knows that. If business leaders and sales professionals would focus on the basics that we are talking about in this book, they will be happy, more effective and successfully, sustainably grow their business. Sustainable success does not come that quickly and must be stuck with, done repetitively over time. Most people want something quicker and easier and especially don't want to have to change themselves (I see lots of leaders that want their people to change but don't want to model the change, admit they don't have all the answers and try to improve themselves).

This excerpt from a Wall Street Journal article, "Executives Must Stop Jumping Fad to Fad and Learn to Manage," by Carol Hymowitz (May 15th, 2006) talks about company leaders following the next movement or idea in management, leadership, or business effectiveness. People jump from one to the other to the other so often that is has become problematic and distracting rather than helpful.

"Consultants make their living trying to convince executives to buy the latest idea in management. These days, there aren't any hot, new trends, just a lot of repackaged ones from the past. Executives have been treated to an overdose of management guides that mostly haven't delivered what they promised. Many bosses have adopted them all, regardless of their company's business model, balance sheet, competition, employee bench strength or any other unique qualities. They have become copycat managers, trying to find a one-stop, fix-it-all answer to their various problems.

Some ideas, of course, will never go out of style. W. Edward Deming's advice to companies to "drive out fear" so managers can act on what they know, admit what they don't know and change decisions that aren't working, is just one example of an idea as relevant today as when first proposed nearly a quarter of a century ago. But even in this case, a 1990s reinvention of Mr. Deming's total-quality movement in manufacturing, called Six Sigma, improved efficiency at scores of plants, but couldn't help companies meet another great need — more innovation.

Executives need to be more skeptical about anything billed as the next big idea. The smartest will learn how to cherry pick what is right for their businesses, rather than follow what they heard about from their golf buddies the previous weekend. Consultants hired by these former employers conducted employee surveys that always produced the same results. Employees would say they wanted more communication. In response, his bosses would say, "Let's put out a newsletter" — missing the message that they wanted to be heard, he says.

An operations manager at a Silicon Valley technology company complains that consultants hired by his bosses produce stunning charts but bungle answers to his production problems. "They tell my superiors we should produce parts only on demand — 1,000 on Monday and 5,000 on Thursday — capacity our suppliers can't handle," he says. Instead of offering complicated analyses, he wishes they'd spend time on the factory floor and understand how equipment really works."

The Oz Principle (excerpt below) also drives this point home. I like the image of pulling back the curtain on the illusion of power and all knowingness that we still sometimes think we have or need to have as leaders, or expect and look for in those that are leading us. We are destined to be disappointed. Recent examples of this in business, politics, and even in our churches show the magnitude of this problem. As our world gets more complex and confusing, we want more of our leaders and they are letting us down as never before.

Or maybe we're just exposing everything behind the curtain — and that's painful, especially when reality is not what we expected. The good news is that we are peeking behind the curtain, exposing our leaders, and also looking at ourselves in an unprecedented fashion in most areas of modern life. We have an opportunity to change what we see, and mostly by changing ourselves, our workplace, and our approach to business, leadership, and sales.

"When you pull back the curtains you discover the "truth" and realize, as did the characters in Oz, that corporate success springs from the willingness of an organization's people to embrace accountability. Too often, however, companies employ the latest management program only to abandon it when an even more up to the minute new program comes along.

...Moving from one illusion of what it takes to achieve organizational effectiveness to another, executives never stop long enough to discover the truth. In reality when you strip away all the trappings, gimmicks, tricks, techniques, methods and philosophies of the latest management "fads" you find them all, albeit awkwardly, striving to accomplish the same thing: to produce greater accountability for results... the essence of organizational success will always be found in the accountable actions and attitudes of individuals."

— Roger Connors, Tom Smith, Craig Hickman, The Oz Principle

Creating an Environment of Trust

In workplace learning environments and regular sales, staff, and leadership meetings, I find most people are afraid to talk about what's not working for them. Simple as it might sound, not enough leaders ask questions about what their teams are struggling with. Sometimes these questions get asked but get no response because people are uncomfortable being honest or it doesn't feel safe to tell the truth. Ideally this kind of truthful exchange can take place without an outside facilitator, although it can be useful to have one present. No matter who's running the meeting, or facilitating the training/learning session or discussion, there are three elements that need to be in place to get to heart of what people are struggling with: Trust, Structure, and Full Engagement.

Trust We all know the best lessons often come from mistakes and failures. And yet we hide our failures, are ashamed of them, and never open up about them in a group forum. For this process to work, there has to be a true sense of value in and credence given to the importance of learning from mistakes, missed opportunities, challenges as much as huge successes. People will only open up and allow themselves to be vulnerable if they trust the leader, if not the entire team. They don't want to be judged, punished, or seen as weak, stupid, or incompetent. If you can create a culture that celebrates and learns from mistakes, as well as successes, you will minimize the repetition of mistakes and increase the opportunities for learning and significant growth, both at an individual and organizational level.

Structure This is a lens from which to view and analyze your failures without it being personal. There has to be a context for mistakes, a framework that helps people make sense of them, and measure their thoughts or actions against. Without a fundamental framework or structure into which everyone has bought into and has clear agreements and expectations around, chaos, lack of accountability, and personalizing mistakes and failures are destined to distract from the end goal. I see a lot of companies that have a "sales process" or "new client engagement process." Each of these has structure in that it has steps — what comes first, what comes next, what to ask, etc. Often times it does not have buy in from those on the front lines with daily opportunities to execute it. I see too many "processes" force-fed with little buy-in from anyone but the leaders who thought it was a good idea. Having a process and a framework to operate from is as much about following key fundamental principles, embodying the right spirit or intent, and having the necessary mental strength as it is about following a step by step map.

"There is often a willingness to leave untouched the most important issues in order to deal objectively with those that can be adequately quantified."
—Theodore Porter as quoted by Jerry Hirshberg
in The Creative Priority

Engagement How many times have you been a part of a meeting or a conference call where you were not fully engaged, just went through the motions, were distracted by random thoughts, or wasted time checking emails? In order to facilitate a discussion that is meaningful and productive, everyone has to be fully present and actively engaged. Easier said than done obviously. There are things you can do, though, to help make this happen. As a leader, I want you to become more aware of the following things. What is and is not working in your weekly management or staff meetings and periodic training sessions? When are people most engaged, or not engaged? Consider some of the topics in this book to mix things up and stimulate some new conversation and level of engagement. Just make sure not to shove any of this material down people's throats. If you do, it will befall the same fate as all your past efforts to integrate "the latest, greatest new system to grow our business!" into your company culture.

How to Change

It's not possible to just think yourself into change. You can't use the same brain that got you here to make a change in your life. You have to be able to observe yourself in order to gain a new and greater perspective. To change, we first must intend the change. Intention results from a conscious decision to change, of your own free will. Change is hard. Therefore, you have to want to change in order to have any success. And I mean really want it. You will find resistance from habitual thoughts in your mind and especially from your ego. The ego hates change, particularly change that minimizes its power and control over you. You will also find resistance from some people in the outside world, at work, and at home. Some will welcome your changes. Many will not. Be prepared for resistance from everywhere. This is another reason why most people need some form of outside support in order to move through these roadblocks and persevere.

Dr. Joe Dispenza says, "What separates us from all other species is the ratio of our *frontal lobe* to the rest of our brain." This is responsible for our decision making, regulating behavior, and creating clear intention. We have the capacity to make choices every day. Choices other animals may not be capable of, we can make in a matter of seconds. With this ability to make clear, conscious choices, and create intentions, also comes the burden of options and the potential to also make an exponential number of bad choices. A dog can make a bad choice to chase a squirrel in front of a moving car, but it's not really even a choice because it is reacting on instinct. We make bad choices while often having full knowledge of the repercussions of our actions.

Our bad choices are often in the form of deciding NOT to do something:

- making a phone call
- going to the gym
- taking a taxi vs. getting in the car to drive home after a few too many drinks
- spending enough time with my best client
- thinking positively, trusting things are going to work out
- valuing myself
- treating others with respect
- being totally honest with a client or business partner

In order to make changes it's essential that the focus and desire to change and do things differently is sustained over time. One of the biggest obstacles to this is that the mind is wandering all over the place. For your new intention to work (i.e.: attract two new "A-caliber" clients before the end of the year) it has to be focused. Yet, at the same time, the culture we're living in is constantly grabbing for our attention. We are inundated daily with marketers' messages for us to pay attention to what's cool and what we must have to be happy. Not to mention our daily barrage of emails, voice mails, phone calls, text messages or IM's, conference calls, meetings, etc. More and more, people are vying for our time and our attention. Your clients

"We all get stuck. Caught in old patterns and habits. The same thoughts keep looping back around. When we are stuck, we are unable to think of anything new."

are experiencing the same thing. It's hard to stay focused and not get distracted.

Pattern Interrupts

Much of what I am referring to is about being able to recognize and interrupt patterns; to move away from — or at least look differently at — the way you've always been doing things. In the specific cases I'm working through, it is related to your process of identifying and engaging more of the right kinds of new clients or growing business from your existing clients. The concept is relevant, of course, in any aspect of your life.

Exercise: Interrupting Our Patterns
(*original author unknown*)

Look briefly at the paragraph below and count the number of F's you see. Write the number down on a piece of paper.

FINISHED FILES ARE THE RE-
SULT OF YEARS OF SCIENTIF-
IC STUDY COMBINED WITH THE
EXPERIENCE OF MANY YEARS

Now, look at the paragraph below. It is identical to the one you just viewed. Again, count the F's. Did you find more of them, less of them, or the same amount? If the number is different this time, write down the number on a piece of paper. If you don't want to cheat and see the answer in advance, don't look below the paragraph. *Answer:* See page 265.

FINISHED FILES ARE THE RE-
SULT OF YEARS OF SCIENTIF-
IC STUDY COMBINED WITH THE
EXPERIENCE OF MANY YEARS

After doing this with groups for a few years, I have found that about ten percent of the time someone sees all six of them on the first try. Thirty percent of the time, someone sees all six of them on the second try. But that leaves a lot of smart, successful, well-educated people that can't count or see the letter F in the above paragraph. How does this happen?

People who don't see all the F's miss the ones in the word "OF." We just skip over it, at least the first time. Our brain is scanning quickly and doesn't even pick those up. For me, achieving new levels of success and results in sales, business, leadership, and life, is about picking up on some of these little details that I've been missing and about looking at things in a different way.

You can notice that at some point, if you keep looking at those paragraphs, you're not getting new results, you're just getting the same repeat loop — like looking in the refrigerator over-and-over and seeing the same thing. You know there is a jar of pickles in there somewhere, but you just can't see it. When we see the same things and think the same thoughts over-and-over, we cement the connections in our brain and build a rut that is hard to get out of.

I know it sounds simple, but I find that you must create new thinking in order to get new, repeatable results. A new way of looking at something, a new perspective, a new approach. William James, often referred to as the father of modern psychology spoke to this quite concisely when he said,

> *"Genius means little more than the faculty*
> *of perceiving in an unhabitual way."*
> —Wayne Dyer, The Power of Intention

Neuroplasticity is the word used to describe the brain's ability to make new connections and change. It's hard to do, but definitely not impossible. I have people that tell me "people can't change." I understand this perspective at a certain level but fundamentally disagree. It's hard for people to change and they have to want to change. There are core, foundational elements of people's personalities and mental programming that are deeply hard wired, yes. So, maybe you can't entirely change who someone is, I agree. But people can create shifts in behaviors, results, and thinking. They just have to be committed, have the right kind of system to support and challenge them, and then continually reinforce the changes to make them stick. I have seen, and do see, people make fundamental shifts in how they act, talk, and think every day. And I'm sure they are not the norm.

> *"People must be encouraged not only to know their craft, their products, their work and the people they serve, but to know a little of themselves. In order to respond to the world of wants, they must know of what they want themselves. Just as important they must know what they do not want. They must look at their inherited fears around conversation, particularly the conversation about their own gifts. The personal conversation can be very frightening, but it is an increasingly necessary one, especially for those who have any leadership role in the organization."*
> —David Whyte, Crossing the Unknown Sea:
> Work as a Pilgrimage of Identity

Slow is Fast - in Sales and Learning

> *"When educating horses, there is no greater maxim than slow is fast and fast is slow. I believe that the groundwork put into developing trust is always worth it, because once trust is established the learning process speeds up noticeably. I call this phenomenon "slow is fast."*
> —Monte Roberts, Horse Sense for People

In sales, if we move too quickly down the line of our process, we often miss essential questions, relevant pieces of information and important cues from the prospect. Sometimes the hardest thing to do is to slow down a prospect who is excited about the idea of working with us. That's when it is the easiest to skip steps in our process and forget to ask key questions. And, sometimes we're working with a difficult prospect who is not giving us all we want or is resisting some questions or next steps, and we get nervous they are going to get mad at us or go away, so we decide to compromise (consciously or unconsciously) and skip some steps or key questions they might not like. There is a natural tendency in sales and business communication for most people to rush things, especially if they are excited and also if they are needy of making something happen. If we move too quickly without the foundation having yet to be laid, we our doing ourselves and the prospect a disservice. The key foundational questions and steps might be different for each person or company, and everyone has them. And they know when they've skipped them and what the consequences are most likely to be. I've done this myself, skipping an entire conversation and moving too quickly to talking about $/price and having a prospect talk to my references. I thought it was a slam dunk. But there were questions that I had not asked yet and data about their challenges and the economics of those challenges and a real compelling reason to change and do something different now. And the prospect got caught up on the money. Basically comparing the cost of my service (i.e.: $20,000) to $0 which is what he was currently paying for the kind of services I was offering. He decided it was too steep a price to pay. My point is that we all move too quickly at times, especially at the beginning of a relationship.

In the context of sales and negotiation, adrenaline is not your friend. Recently, a client sent me this note after he had a realization how the emotion he thought was helping him and just a part of the process of sales, was actually keeping him

from closing business. He saw how he was getting too attached
— wanting the deal more than the prospective clients wanted
help or change. And how even when things were going well,
if he got too excited about things, his prospects would start
backing off, or would later change their mind. This might
seem counter-intuitive to what you've been taught or learned
in sales. You might not even agree. I happen to believe this
statement is quite prescient and right on the money.

> *"Intense emotion in a sales situation, no matter how*
> *well-intentioned seems to more often than not have an*
> *undesired outcome, and leaves you feeling drained as well."*
> — Brian Frampton, Sales Professional

Key Reminders:

- Get off the bandwagon. The next "big thing" business
  initiative or quick fix is not going to get to the heart of
  the matter to create real change.

- You have to want to change. You have to want to do
  something different; to be motivated and courageous
  about trying new things, and making mistakes.

- Slow is fast in learning (and in your sales process).
  If things are moving too fast, you will lose control of
  your ability to retain information and make sustained
  changes over time. The same goes for your new client
  engagement process. If things are moving too fast (even
  if that seems like a good thing), slow it down.

COURAGE

Preview Points:

- Face fear, discomfort, and the unknown head on – you will reap the rewards, and it will get easier every time.

- Your desire for "safety," while reasonable and understandable, holds you back.

- Your thoughts and actions must be congruent in order to create profoundly different and sustainable results.

"When one has nothing to lose, one becomes courageous.
We are timid only when there is something we can still cling to."
— Carlos Casteneda

Facing Fear & Discomfort Head-On

The Roman philosopher Tacitus said, "The desire for safety stands against every great and noble enterprise." Our ability to tolerate discomfort and the unknown often leads to the most significant breakthroughs.

As we get older and more have more successes, we often become more timid. Executing the approaches I have suggested in this book is not easy. They take time, discipline, commitment, and the perseverance to break through deep seated habits. To really "do" what I have outlined day in and day out takes real courage. A good friend sent me this story when I was looking for some inspiration. I return to it whenever I need to summon courage or inspire others to take what feel like big risks.

Burn your Boats at the Shore

(author unknown)

April of 1519 when Cortes lands in Veracruz, about 200 miles from the Aztec capital. Cortes had a singular mission: defeat the Aztecs and take their gold. To do so, he had less than 400 soldiers, 16 horses, 14 pieces of artillery, 11 ships, plenty of guns and ammunition, and cajones. His first act upon landing was to burn all but one of his ships — he wanted no turning back.

He told the Spanish Governor about his plan to help Spain get roots in the "New World." The Spanish Governor was so excited that he gave this man eleven ships and seven hundred men to assure the voyage's success.

Hernando Cortez indeed had a plan. The only problem is that the plan he shared with the Spanish Governor and his "true plan" were not exactly identical. He had one wrinkle to throw into the plan that he shared with nobody. Cortez wasn't convinced that eleven ships and seven hundred men would guarantee his success. So, after months of sailing, he landed on the shore of Veracruz in the Spring of 1519 and implemented plan "la."

Plan "la" went as follows: Burn the ships! That's right! After he had safely landed in Mexico, he ordered the men to burn the ships.

Survival is our most primitive instinct. Cortez didn't know the strength of the men he would be fighting. He had no idea of the dangers facing him and his men. But he did know one thing. If the fighting got too difficult, and the way became too frightening, there would be no talk of returning to Veracruz and sailing home.

Patience, fortitude, and focus are also words that, to me, are synonymous with courage. This includes being able to persevere, continuing to adjust when necessary, and staying the course when it's the right thing to do. Too often we equate courage with ego and forcefulness. For every high-ego leader on the front page of a magazine or newspaper, there are thousands more who are successful, full of integrity, and have the courage to follow their path in the face of criticism and distraction. There are no quick fixes in business, especially in sales. The upgrading of your skills takes time and commitment. Are you going to quit when things get hard or when you don't see an immediate spike in sales after two weeks of trying these new approaches? Bestselling author Marcus Buckingham, in his book *The One Thing You Need to Know*, speaks of the phrase "self-efficacy" as even more important than self-esteem. They are both useful, and when push comes to shove, just having a high regard and sense of yourself does not necessarily translate into the kind of focus, commitment and courage that you will need to get to the next level in your career.

"Self-efficacy is not the same as self esteem. Self esteem refers to your general feeling of worthiness, and, while having high esteem must, in some general sense, be a good thing, a recent APS study revealed that high self esteem predicts nothing at all — not resilience, not persistence, not goal-setting, and certainly not achievement... Your level of self efficacy for an activity does an excellent job of predicting your subsequent performance. It predicts how quickly you will bounce back from failure at the activity, how forcefully you will persevere at the activity when you meet obstacles or setbacks, how high your goals for that activity will be, and, most important of all, the likelihood you will actually achieve these goals. When it comes to performance, self-efficacy is one of the most powerful of mental states."
— Marcus Buckingham, The One Thing You Need to Know

Finding your Center

When playing any sort of sales or business development role most professionals will find themselves at one time or another at extreme ends of the spectrum in their approach, ranging from overly passive to overly aggressive. Sometimes you might come on too strong, full of ego, self-protection, and masking your attachment with phrases like, "If they can't see that this is a no-brainer, screw 'em!" On the flipside, some business professionals are overly passive with their sales and networking efforts, avoiding certain essential activities that are a little out of their comfort zone.

It takes an enormous amount of energy to *hold it all together*, especially if you or your team are out of alignment. I have met company leaders and middle managers who find themselves in way over their heads and have to work ten times harder to keep up in fear of being labeled as ineffective, unintelligent, or outright frauds. I have worked with business leaders who have virtually no passion for the business they are in and the work they do. They are trapped, trying to make the most of it, while not asking themselves the hard questions. I have seen countless sales professionals who love selling and enjoy people but hate their manager, their organization, or the product / service they are selling (or at worst, all three). They stick around in order to get paid, but operate at well below their maximum capabilities. Or they jump from sales job to sales job, never really finding congruence between their passions and the areas in which they have the most talent.

Congruence (*noun*): Agreement, harmony, conformity, or correspondence.

We all have really good sensors for judging when something is just not right. We often ignore that voice, or if we do listen to it, don't know how to either turn things around in our favor or respectfully walk away. Notice confusion and when something doesn't feel right in a sales situation or important negotiation. Notice when you are feeling excitement that seems premature. Notice anything that doesn't seem to fit the situation or seem genuine. Develop what a friend of mine calls your *spidey-sense*. This *spidey-sense* will serve you well and be one more way to give you the upper hand. Not the upper hand so you can manipulate others, but so you can facilitate a process that you control, that allows your prospects the best possible chance to get their problem solved, and puts you in the best position to win the deal if you are the vendor that can best solve their problems.

Often when we talk about congruence, we are also talking about being radically honest with ourselves and with others. So much of the talk in corporate America is fake and lacking a genuine and truly effective exchange. People are so afraid to say the wrong thing or piss someone off that they hide behind buzzwords and false concern. Many get too attached to a particular outcome that keeps them from saying anything that might rock the boat. I'm not suggesting you be outspoken for the sake of rocking the boat and throwing people off center. I am definitely not suggesting or encouraging anyone to intimidate or manipulate others. I do find that most business professionals know what they want to say and what the next step needs to be in their sales process. They just needed a little reminder and some courage to go ahead and say it, ask for it, or propose that next step. It sounds so simple, I know. We all get stuck at times, though, thanks to our ego and the diet of fear and doubt it tries to feed us.

One of my colleagues was telling me about a consultant he had recently met with, hoping to do some networking and discuss a possible strategic alliance. As a part of our network, we're always looking for mutually beneficial business partnerships and we have certain filters we run everyone through, certain red flags we're watching for. Congruence on a personal level and on a business level are on the top of the list. My colleague made the following comment, which really stood out to me. "Funny... he told me a key aspect of his business is that he helps clients establish prospect lists and more effectively work these lists to increase new business. When I asked him some more questions about his business, he shared with me that his biggest challenge was prospecting!"

Play a Bigger Game, Change the Playing Field

Striving for business growth, professional success, and increased results is about finding ways to "play a bigger game" in how and where you focus your mindset and approach to business growth. It doesn't take MORE time to call higher in an organization, ensuring you're talking to the person that has to most to lose or gain from your solution. Make sure you're talking to those that control budgets, can make big decisions, and can think and make decisions outside of the day to day box of what they're "supposed to do." It doesn't take MORE energy to identify and focus on life changing, ideal clients. It isn't actually HARDER to talk more honestly and transparently with clients, or to ask really good questions.

Get dissatisfied with incrementalism, mediocrity, and the status quo.

Most spend too much time playing small, chasing their tails, and doing more of the same thing. This is because of unconsciousness (i.e.: lack of awareness), fear and often some kind of twisted addiction to struggle and things being "hard." To actually "play a bigger game", there is a great deal of reprogramming that has to happen at an organizational, team, and individual level. You must make fundamental shifts to your Thinking about yourself and your business, your Language in prospecting and negotiating, and your Process for engaging new clients and growing business within existing ones. In order to do this, there has to be a consistent, disciplined focus on this kind of change over a period of time.

> *"To grow your business and your income, you must always be seeking larger opportunities. Be willing to move on from the smaller ones. Stay active looking for more of the right kinds of new business and letting go of the "C" prospects and clients. This takes both faith and courage."*

I had a friend who was a very successful entrepreneur, becoming a millionaire by age 30. He told me once that he doesn't work any harder or have more hours in the day than most people. It's just that he attacks bigger problems and has the courage to call the president of a billion dollar company to get a meeting to discuss a big idea he has to make them money. He's talking to people that can make big decisions and take significant risks. He's working on $100 million problems and opportunities. Doing this takes more vision and courage. It does not take more time.

Key Reminders:

- Burn your boats at the shore. Make courageous commitments where there
  is no going back. Lead by example.
- Self efficacy (how well you bounce back from failure) not self esteem (sense of worth) most determines results.
- Play a bigger game. Thinking big and being courageous doesn't take more time.

DESIRE FOR MEANING

Preview Points:

- Quantum leaps result from attaching day-to-day focus with a larger, transformational goal and intention.
- Even the most mundane jobs have a larger purpose.
- We are all looking to feel connected and for a sense of purpose. If not, what's the point?

Finding Meaning at Work

Why do you do what you do? What's the draw to your current profession, career, place of work? Why this business, this profession, this company? Do you really care about what you are selling, and the service you are providing? Do you really care about your clients? I know you work to make money, but beyond that why do you do what you do?

These questions are not nec-essarily designed to be prickly, judgmental or stir up a deep soul searching session. This book of course has been about how to more effectively grow your client base and your business. I am not suggesting that you must relate your role at work or running your business to some altruistic calling that helps to save the world. However, I do want to challenge you to make sure you understand why you do what you do – beyond the paycheck. There has to be some kind of bigger point to it all, or some additional joy you get out of

> *"Quantum leaps in your results happen when you attach your day to day focus to a larger, transformational goal."*

the process of what you do on a day-to-day basis. Even if it's purely capitalistic, that's fine, as long as you're enjoying it, providing value to others, and getting well paid. You don't have to be working on a cure for AIDS or cancer for your life to have purpose and meaning. You could be selling cemetery plots to the aging or software to retail shops and find some sense of purpose. What is it that you most enjoy about what you do? What gets you out of bed every morning?

"The antidote for exhaustion is not rest. It is wholeheartedness."
—David Whyte

I suggest that it might be possible for you to throw yourself more whole-heartedly into your current professional role. And if you just can't do it, then you should consider moving on to something else. It is not my intent to get you to quit your job. Sometimes the courageous thing is to stay where you are, re-engage, and find a way to try and make it work for you and those around you. I would ask you to ask yourself, "Am I really giving it my all?" Given what you've read in this book, I imagine you can find elements of this approach that you can try differently related to your **Thinking, Language,** and **Process** for growing your business, and yourself. I imagine that if you are in a leadership role there are ways you can attempt to influence change within your team or entire organization. What might that look like if you were to get radically honest with yourself and those around you in a way that you have not done before? Consider that the material in this book is an opportunity to do things differently and engage in your work life at a whole different level. And that it will also spill over and relate to your personal life as well.

Q: What do you find salespeople, business professionals most struggle with today?

A: "Finding meaning in their work. I haven't found too many people who don't want some fulfillment beyond a paycheck, yet that's all most people seem to get from their work."

— Bryan Neale, Business Owner / Sales Consultant

We are all trying to connect with others, and to feel valued and appreciated. We all like to help others and appreciate it when others provide us support. We want to know that we are good. The sales, negotiation, and business communication process is driven by these fundamental needs. Of course, there is business to do which is important. That being said, the separation from our personal and professional self is not nearly as significant as some people think it is, or try to make it. The better we can understand these basic human drives, the more human a face we can put on our prospective new clients. They are just people. The more psychologically savvy we can be about understanding our clients and ourselves, the more effective we can be at finding the right kind of business partnerships. Subsequently, we can spend less time Barking Up Wrong Trees and Beating Dead Horses. Integrating this approach making it second nature to your day to day interactions is hard work and in many ways is never finished. Because this is true and some don't like it, they continue to search for the quick fix, the silver bullet, the one golden path to riches and eternal bliss.

Q: What do you find salespeople, business professionals most struggle with today?

A: "From my perspective, sales and business people are searching for meaning, purpose, and worth in their careers, but are not sure how to attain these and incorporate them into their daily lives."

—Geoff Leech, Sales Executive

Having a level of caring for your people, your product/ service, your company, and your clients is something that differentiates happy professionals from those that are stressed and depressed. One of the most important elements to full engagement from a sales team, account service team, project management team, etc. is trust and care. I have had the pleasure to work with a number of successful, healthy organizations where there is a core theme throughout. The employees, agents, and reps feel the company, it's leadership and their boss in particular, care about them and are looking out for their best interest.

"A multitude of research studies confirm that employees are more productive when they feel that someone at work cares about them. Actually, the research confirms more than the casual link between caring and productivity. It also reveals that employees who feel cared about are less likely to miss workdays, less likely to have accidents on the job, less likely to file workers' compensation claims, less likely to steal, less likely to quit and more likely to advocate for the company to friends and family. No matter how you choose to measure performance, being cared about seems to drive it."
—Marcus Buckingham, The One Thing You Need to Know

I'm not suggesting that group hugs, trust falls, and sessions for sharing your feelings need to be integrated into your management process. I am suggesting too many leaders discount the importance of caring. The more you genuinely show you care for others, the more of the right kinds of people you will attract and the happier they will be.

Once, when helping a client with a brainstorming session about their unique value, we boiled it down to a tagline that they unfortunately couldn't use on their website or in their PowerPoints, and yet is woven into the culture, "We give a sh--." In other words, they care. They do good work, are responsive, thoughtful, and smart. They don't claim they won't make mistakes, but they do say they will find and admit them quickly, and then create a plan to fix them. I think that most people are very reasonable. They don't expect you (or your company) to be perfect. They do expect you to be accountable, try your best, communicate well, and be responsive and fair. It's not rocket science. Many of our American companies, leaders, and politicians could use a reminder of this. Caring goes a long way, and it's not something you can fake.

Key Reminders:

- What is the point? Tap into a larger goal for yourself, your team, or your organization.
- People are more productive when they feel someone at work (their boss in particular) cares about them and has their best interest at heart.
- We are all looking for a sense of purpose.

CONCLUSION

This book will be most useful if you take its contents to heart and weave it into your daily routine over time. I trust you will be able to take some of the key points and generate tangible results for yourself and your team. Below are a few key reminders I'd like to leave you with.

Authenticity Sells

Today, more than ever, people are looking for more genuine and authentic brands to purchase, and thoughtful, honest, and effective new business partnerships to forge. Everyone is very busy. People are overwhelmed and are tired of b.s. They want business relationships they can trust, that add value, that can be measured at the bottom line, and that are also interesting, challenging, and rewarding at a personal and professional level. People are responding to a more human, authentic approach.

> *"Integrity - Authenticity comes to a brand that is what it says it is. In other words, the story that the brand tells through its actions aligns with the story it tells through its communications. Only then will customers sense that the brand's story is true."*
> —Bill Breen, Fast Company Magazine, May 2007,
> The Appeal and Risks of Authenticity

What We Call "Selling" Isn't Really Selling Any More

Your job is to engage people in conversations and help them figure out what they need and if you can help them. We often make "sales" or "business development" out to be this big THING. When we make it a THING, it keeps us from making that call, asking for that referral, having that lunch, or calling that lead. This mindset leads to avoidance and the most dangerous thing for any business — lack of consistent, growth-related activity. There are ways to make new business development more comfortable, human, and not so much of a THING. It can be comfortable, easy, and even kind of fun with the right approach. You can show the client that you are the expert without having to feel like you are "selling."

The better you understand your unique value - what you do naturally well that your clients most value - and the more effectively you communicate it, the more people you will help and the more you will get paid.

You have the opportunity to control the client engagement process. He who has the most effective and disciplined process, wins. Your process for engaging prospects is an opportunity to differentiate yourself from the competition.

The more quickly you weed out and let go of bad prospects, the quicker you can find new and better ones. This takes a focused effort to find more new prospects, while simultaneously spending less time on drawn out, lingering deals with people that are not really ready to do business with you.

"No" is perfectly ok. The one thing traditional selling NEVER does is to make "no" perfectly ok. The truth is, the answer is often no: "No, we're not open to talk right now," "No, we're not interested in what you do," etc. If we make no an ok answer at every stage in our process, while also doing a better job with how we communicate our unique value, we create the space for them to say yes when that might not be their normal, first response. This is the paradox of it all — we have to make no ok in order to give ourselves a better chance of getting a yes. And if the answer is really no, then I want to know that too. The first job in trying to generate new business from new prospects and existing clients is to get a response. And the second is to get the truth.

No begging. What most would argue is just being polite, actually puts anyone working on getting new business in a one-down position, beneath their client. I ask all my clients to delete the word "please" from all the prospecting and business development communication. This is a weak word. Same goes for "Thanks for your time." Most people have a hard time with both of these. The problem is you're setting up the dynamic that their time is MORE valuable than yours - which is not true. You have unique value and possible solutions to their problems. You can save them time and make them more money, not to mention make their life easier and more productive. Your time and energy is of equal value to your prospect and client's. Act, and talk, like it.

No assumptions. It may seem radical, but, in my opinion, you should not assume that you can help everyone. You're really seeing if a prospect is OPEN to your help. You think you can help them, but until you have an idea of what they are struggling with, looking to achieve, and open to - and then seeing if those things are in alignment with what you do and how you do it - you can't be sure. Any words or phrases that are used before you really know a prospect that give the impression that you are assuming you can help (i.e.: "I am excited about the ways we can help you.") or assuming that they will call you back (i.e.: "I look forward to hearing back from you."), minimizes your chances of advancing your process and creating the space for an open dialogue.

"I don't know," is perfectly fine, and can actually be a strong statement. In sales and negotiation "I don't know" is a dirty word that almost no one uses. If it's true, and is delivered in the right way and context, it can actually put you in a position of strength and increases your chances of getting the truth. Out of context, this can sound a bit crazy, I'm sure. Again, all this is designed to help get the truth, ensure the sales process progresses, and stay in control. In every situation, there are things you KNOW (data - irrefutable fact) and things you DON'T KNOW (but might be interested to find out). If you think it, say it. Be refreshingly honest and you will stand out from the crowd and waste less time with people that are not a good fit for you or your organization.

Mindset of abundance vs. scarcity. You have an abundant marketplace of opportunity. There are plenty of people that are in need of your product or service. If you think anything other than this on a daily basis, you are costing yourself a lot of money. Your mindset sets up your ability to attract more of the right kinds of clients. Pay attention to your thoughts to see if they are running through an abundance or scarcity filter.

Shift in Self-Perception

Besides the strategies and tactics in this book, one theme that I have tried to convey is the importance of creating a shift in the perception you have of yourself. New business development related activities provide a unique opportunity to see yourself differently; to face your fears and try new ways of interacting with clients. The bonus here is that as you get better at these things, you will see more financial success, solve more problems, and help more people. The goal for this book has been to plant some seeds in your head and give you a few tools for how you might interrupt some old, habitual patterns and see yourself and your business in a whole new way.

I wish you continued abundance and that your hard work becomes a little more effortless. I trust that you are clearer now than ever before about more effective approaches to growing your revenue and profitability, while spending less time and energy barking up wrong trees and beating dead horses.

"The realities of the world beyond our lilypads are changing as never before. The choice is ours: Do we become visionaries? Or do we just sit around the pond wondering what happened to all the flies?"
— Philip Slater, *The Wayward Gate*
(as quoted in *The Way of Adventure* by Jeff Salz)

Join the Conversation

I am interested in what principles and key points have been most useful for you. What have you been able to practice and see results from? What questions do you have about the material and its application? What kind of meaningful shifts have you been able to make in your thinking, your language, or your process?

Join the conversation at: www.perficency.com/barking

RECOMMENDED READING

Below are a few books that have recently influenced me, my writing, and teaching. This is not a comprehensive list, but gives you a couple of "out-of-the-sales-box" ideas for business and personal growth. I find that NOT reading sales books is what has helped me make quantum leaps in my sales results and those of my clients. If you are a thoughtful, growth-oriented professional, I encourage you to branch out in what you read. Make new, relevant connections to other creative ideas and perspectives that might help you be more effective in your approach to growing your business and yourself.

- Marcus Buckingham, *The One Thing You Need to Know... About Great Management, Great Leadership & Sustained Individual Success.*
- Malcolm Gladwell, *Blink*
- Eckhart Tolle, *The Power of Now + A New Earth*
- Susan Scott, *Fierce Conversations*
- Bill Caskey, *Same Game, New Rules*
- Wayne Dyer, *The Power of Intention*
- Thomas Friedman, *The World is Flat*
- Monty Roberts, *Horse Sense for People*
- David Hawkins, *Power vs. Force*
- David Whyte, *The Heart Aroused + Crossing the Unknown Sea: Work as a Pilgrimage of Identity*
- Patrick Lencioni, *The Five Dysfunctions of a Team*

- Victor Frankl, *Man's Search for Meaning*
- Napoleon Hill, *Think and Grow Rich*
- Stuart Wilde, *The Little Money Bible + Silent Power*
- William Arntz, Betsy Chasse, Mark Vicente, *What the BLEEP Do We Know!?*
- Jerry Hirshberg, *The Creative Priority*
- Jeff Salz, *The Way of Adventure*
- Michael Lewis, *Moneyball*
- Fast Company Magazine

GLOSSARY OF KEY TERMS USED

Intent: The underlying reason, purpose, motivation, tone, and focus of your conversation. i.e.: "What is your intent for calling Joe. What is it that you want to come out of this call?" By exploring the intent behind the action, we are better able to understand the underlying thinking the individual has and explore any gaps or red flags that we may be able to correct before the action is taken. To increase and change results, exploring one's thinking and underlying intent is everything. All results and changes flow from here.

Value: The intrinsic or transactional worth of an individual, organization or particular offering of goods or services. The foundation of the work we do is built upon the concept and belief that most individuals and organizations don't fully understand, believe in, or effectively communicate their value. Getting yourself and your organization more meaningfully connected to your value (both in the personal, emotional realm and in the business, transactional realm) is the only way to get paid more for what you do. Thinking about it differently and talking about it differently will lead to different results.

Thinking: The psychology of your thoughts (and also underlying emotions). What's going on in your head that drives your actions. We all have "default" beliefs about others and ourselves that lead to assumptions and compulsive actions (done reactively, without conscious thought). The only way to change these actions, if in fact a person or organization is interested in change, is to first understand the thinking behind the actions. Second, one must work to make changes in this thinking. This is the only path toward sustainable change. This involves both the personal and professional self. This involves taking a hard look in the mirror and is not for the faint of heart. This involves doing work over time (six – twenty four months) in order to ensure the "stickiness" of the changes and trans-formational results (both tangible bottom line and intangible humanistic ones).

Language: Words are everything. Especially in the age of email, voice mail, and virtual meetings, your words can make or break you. Focusing more carefully on your words is another way to separate yourself from the competition, get more results from less effort, and attract the right kinds of clients. In the new client engagement process, existing client negotiation process, or conflict resolution process - internally or with clients - your words are your primary asset. There are words and phrases we have identified that are most helpful to keep a client or prospect open to hear you out ("I'm pretty sure you have no idea who I am. Let me tell you quickly why I'm calling") and to help you keep control ("what I've found works best" / "as a part of my process"); words NOT to use when you are in negotiation or resolving a conflict with a client or employee ("those are all great points, BUT...."); and words and phrases we don't typically use that we should to help move a sales process forward ("This is what I know. This is what I DON'T know." / "I have no idea" / "I'm not sure"). Your language is the first translation of the intent (along with the tone and cadence of your voice via phone and body language when face-to-face). Executing this well will allow you to keep your clients opened up, telling you the truth, and trusting you.

Process: The system that you have developed (consciously or unconsciously) around anything. In this case we are interested in your process for engaging with new prospective clients. We are also interested in your process for engaging with and growing business from current clients. And finally, your process for dealing with problems, concerns, and conflicts with existing clients, new prospects, and internal staff (bosses, employees or peers). What steps do you take. What comes before what. And lastly, what your core "guiding principles" are that are fueling and providing the backbone for your process (i.e.: "the customer is always right" / "we are only interested in 'A' clients").

Ideal Client: Based upon the principle that "you attract what you define", the Ideal Client is a list of tangible and intangible criteria to describe your ideal clients. The clearer and more detailed this list is, the more often you are talking about it (i.e.: integrating it into your conversations with clients about referrals) and looking at the words and envisioning these people / this organization, the more likely you are to attract them. The flip side is that "you get more of what you tolerate." It has been our experience most organizations have not spent much (if any) time looking at who their A-B-C clients are, what percentage of time they spend on each, and what percentage of their business (revenue and profit) comes from each. The better we understand these numbers and the kinds of clients we'd like to have MORE OF, the more likely we are to attract clients that are fun and easy to work with and also return more revenue and profit to our organization, not to mention to refer more "like-minded" prospects.

Detachment: The more "attached" we are to a particular outcome, the more likely we are to NOT get what we want. The more self serving our attachment is, the lower the odds of us getting the deal done. Detachment keeps us in control of our own emotions (staying one step behind the prospect or client), by not getting too excited, needy, or scared. Being detached does not mean not caring. It does mean not caring more about things than your prospect or client and not being so self serving about your own needs that you are blind to what's truly best for them. Detachment takes emotional discipline and balance. The less needy you are for the business, the more you come from a place of high intent of facilitating a conversation/process to help them decide what's best for them, and are truly ok with any decision (yes or no), the more detached you are and the more business will come your way. People want to be around and do business with people that care about them, that they trust, that are competent, and that don't NEED their business. This is a fundamental principle that is essential to new and sustainable breakthrough results.

Abundance: Seeing the opportunity in all situations. Trusting that your needs will and can get met. Seeing there are plenty of people / organizations that need what you have and that are willing to pay you for it. Understanding your value enough and having had enough experience to see, feel, and know that business has, does, and will come your way.

Scarcity: Driven by fear and a lack of trust. Seeing the negative side of situations, and actively looking for it. Fear that your needs will not get met, that there is not enough money (or time, energy, love, etc.) to go around, especially for you and/or your organization.

Lingering Deal: A deal / negotiation / sales situation where things are "on the fence." Not sure what the next step is, not sure where the client / prospect is 'at'. They are not in a yes "bucket" and they are not in a no "bucket." Lingering situations abound in sales and are very costly. The more effective we can be at quickly getting people into or out of our process, the better. Often times, emotion (fear, attachment) comes into play that causes lingering deals. Often times it is poor or unclear process (or defaulting to "their" process) that leads go lingering deals. The objective when looking at a lingering deal is two-fold. First is understanding how we got here and identifying any red flags we missed or gaps in our process that we can learn from. Secondly, is taking action to re-engage with client / prospect to move them towards some action — either moving forward into your process or moving themselves out of your process. In order to get "the truth" here, the key is to be "detached" and OK with either one. Clarity and the ability to put them in a bucket an move them in or out is the most important thing here. "On the fence" is very costly to your time and energy and also costs you Money.

Pain: The problems, issues, challenges, struggles that a prospect is feeling, going through that you can help them solve.

Opportunity: The possibilities you can help your prospect connect to. The ways in which you do (with clients) and can (with prospects who are open to it) help them achieve a new and better reality.

Selling 180: Reference to the 180-degree reframe from the old way of looking at sales (the buyer has control) to a more progressive approach (where you have equal control) to the prospect / project engagement process.

Upfront Frame: How we begin each conversation, especially one that involves business development, negotiations or new client engagement processes. Starting out each conversation with an understanding of the agreements.

- Why we are here? (what the intent is and what we will be doing)
- How much time we have and any other logistical agreements.
- Tee them up for questions (if you'll be asking them questions) and open yourself up to the same.
- Talk about what will happen at the end of the meeting (go-no go).
- Get confirmation and agreement from all parties before moving forward.

This is designed for optimum efficiency and also to give yourself the best chance to have an honest, open, truthful dialogue.

Red Flag: The situations during your client engagement process where you are looking for words, phrases, responses, actions, situational realities that would cause you to pause and re-examine, ask more questions, etc. BEFORE moving forward. Looking back upon a failed client engagement process, we also look back and ask what "red flags" we missed.

Radical Honesty (aka "Being thoughtfully, radically honest") – Being direct and honest with people about your feelings, concerns, etc. Doing so in a respectful way, without being personal and hurtful with your comments. Speaking of your own observations, concerns, etc. that you feel must be addressed. Bringing up the things you are often most afraid to say. And doing it with high intent (see above) and motive. Speaking the truth. Asking for more truth, with the goal of a more productive and meaningful conversation.

Congruence: *Actual definitions; the quality or state of agreeing, coinciding, in agreement, harmonious, consistent elements, similar, like, amicable, in concert, evenly balanced, symmetrical, corresponding.* Do your actions match your words? Those that I have worked with that are the most successful follow a few key principles that direct and focus their effort and their thinking in all situations. Those that struggle are lacking a framework or filter through which to run their life and their actions. Or, some have a framework that looks and sounds one way on the surface but the reality of it is something different entirely.

Qualities of Top Performers
in Sales & Professional Services

Open to learning
A student of learning. No matter how successful, always open to new ideas and ways to improve. Open to direct and honest feedback.

Master of their process
Has a complete process and executes it daily. Has process for engaging new clients, getting referrals from existing clients, system for administrative support and paperwork, process for scheduling and life balance. The more systemized, the more sustainably successfully without burnout.

Motivated by more than money
Some level of passion for what they do. Eager to take on the challenge of building something, being the best and providing more value to more clients.

Work seems effortless
Feeling like you're doing something that you're good at. Where you feel very well compensated for the value you bring and it comes naturally to you.

Sees the marketplace as abundant
Even in hard times, has the ability to see the opportunities in the marketplace. Is resilient and optimistic without being naive. Believes in self and trusts their process will deliver results in any business climate.

Has prospects convincing them that they are prospects

Doesn't "push", but "pulls." Sets the stage with clarity and conviction, but is respectfully detached from the individual outcomes and lets the prospect do the work.

Is not afraid the ask the tough questions

Fearless without arrogance, is able to ask difficult questions, risk being judged, and making people uncomfortable. Able to do this and still keep the people psychologically "OK" enough to stay engaged, challenge assumptions, and open to change.

Quickly creates an environment of safety and trust

Frames the sales process and meeting clearly and quickly to keep client feeling safe and ok to open up.

Understands their value and connects it to prospect's pain

Frames their value in real world terms that are specific and relevant to the prospect and their current pain or potential opportunities. Does so at a gut level without using buzzwords.

Curious, looks to solve problems, and unattached to outcomes

Has a natural curiosity, asks great questions, interested in solving problems, and is not attached to specific outcomes of individual meetings.

Fearlessly resilient

Undeterred by adversity. Stays the course with focus and passion.

QUALITIES OF TOP PERFORMERS
IN SALES & PROFESSIONAL SERVICES

Clear and passionate about what they do and why they do it
Tells a compelling and personal story about who they are and why they believe in what they do, why they do it, and who they do it for. Shows passion and conviction without too much excitement. Compels people to want to follow them and be a part of what they have going on.

Does not take "No" personally
Learns to check ego's needs at the door and be ok with "No." Does not feel the need to push people to outcomes they are not ready for. Is OK challenging people, but knows the line between challenging, asking, and then convincing and persuading. Understands that "No" is not a personal attack.

Has a high regard for their own personal value
With a healthy balance, has a deep understanding and belief in the value of who they are (as a human) and the skills and gifts they bring to the table as a professional. Belief in themselves and what they do in a grounded and confident way.

Qualities of Top Performers
in Sales Leadership

Vision
Define the future in vivid terms, through their actions, words, images. Leave no doubt where they and their team are headed.

Clear expectations
Ensuring their team understands what is expected of them, individually and collectively. Using consistent check-ins to eliminate ambiguity and minimize potential swings in performance and focus.

Self-efficacy
How quickly they bounce back from failure or set backs. Perseverance.

Balanced emotional attachment
Caring is important, with employees, internal organizational challenges and high stakes sales situations. However, caring TOO much, or more than others, is a recipe for unnecessary stress.

Coaching instinct
Being genuinely intrigued by their people and their unique talents and the challenge of figuring out how to arrange things so that they can experience the greatest success possible. Having passion for "Helping other people grow."

QUALITIES OF TOP PERFORMERS
IN SALES LEADERSHIP

Trust
Their people trust them and believe they have their best interest at heart. Their words and actions are congruent with each other.

Self aware
Have worked to better understand their compulsive habits, patterns, and mindsets that can hold them back. Able to "own" certain behaviors and not make everyone else the problem. Able and willing to take a hard look in the mirror, especially in difficult or charged situations.

Open to experiment
Not afraid of taking chances and risking failure. Passion for trying new things. High "courage quotient." Curious and inquisitive, always on the lookout for the small insight or new perspective that gives them an edge in the marketplace.

Driven
Passion for building something. Desire to succeed and make money. Able to celebrate victories and acknowledge progress, while at the same time never quite being satisfied. The *rub* between the *what is* and the *what could be* motivates them.

Genuine
Having a natural, genuine nature is essential to inspiring others sustainably. Being transparent, honest, clear, real, and authentically HUMAN.

Curious
Excellent at asking questions and active listening. Natural curiosity that cannot be faked. Seeks to understand problems and people before jumping to conclusions.

QUALITIES OF TOP PERFORMERS
IN SALES LEADERSHIP

Sales abilities
Still open to get "in the trenches." Not above selling, making calls, etc. Modeling key mindsets and behaviors for your team. Progressive thinker and communicator, staying up to date on new ideas and approaches to sales communication. Comfort with email, phone, and face-to-face communication with prospects.

Process oriented
Ability to execute key processes on a consistent basis. Disciplined ability to stay focused and follow through with weekly meetings, team one-on-ones, reporting, tracking, etc.

Ability to rally people to a better future
Carrying a vivid image of what the future could be. Ability to clearly and effectively communicate their own image of the future and get people to buy into that image.

Optimistic
A sincere, deep belief that things can get better. This does not mean being unrealistic, nor does it mean always being positive and full of sunshine. It does mean that nothing can undermine their faith that things will improve.

Approachable
Pleasant demeanor. Approachable and fair-minded. Not necessary to be everyone's friend, but important to earn their respect and have an overall positive disposition.

Open to feedback
Interested in seeking feedback from employees, peers, and boss or board. This may be in a formal, structured process or done more informally. The key being open to and interested in feedback.

If you would like information about in-house corporate training and consulting programs, high-level private coaching, public workshops, or speaking engagements, you can visit www.perficency.com or contact Ray Green at 760-402-6285, ray.green@perficency.com. If you have questions or comments for me, I can be reached directly at tom@perficency.com.

Answer to brain teaser on page 225: There are six F's.

Breinigsville, PA USA
04 August 2010
243008BV00001BC/152/A